# THE APPRENTICESHIP OF BEING HUMAN

Why Early Childhood Parenting Matters to Everyone

Graham Scharf

"It is easier to build strong children than to repair broken men."
Frederick Douglass

Printed in the United States of America

First Printing, 2013

www.ApprenticeshipOfBeingHuman.com

Dedicated to:
Elisabeth and Katherine, for the privilege of being your father

# TABLE OF CONTENTS

INTRODUCTION .................................................................11

    Questions, Questions, Questions ......................................12

    The Gap.............................................................................14

CHAPTER 1  Apprenticeship.............................................19

CHAPTER 2  What's the Big Deal? ...................................22

    The Education Crisis ........................................................22

    The Parenting Gap..........................................................23

    The Fathering Gap..........................................................24

    Toward a Tipping Point...................................................25

CHAPTER 3  Brain Building: Birth to 5 ..........................27

    Parents Can Cause Brain Damage...................................28

    Normal & Normative.......................................................30

    Practice Makes (Almost) Permanent...............................31

CHAPTER 4  Scripted: The Role of Stories .....................35

    Indwelling........................................................................36

    Initiation .........................................................................38

    Indoctrination .................................................................38

CHAPTER 5  Clever Devils: Why Virtue Trumps Test Scores .39

    Character .........................................................................39

    Competence .....................................................................41

    Creativity.........................................................................41

    Collaboration ..................................................................42

CHAPTER 6  Cultivating Character...................................44

    Routines & Rudiments ....................................................44

    Poverty of Language........................................................45

Practice & Perseverance.................................................46

The Hothouse of Brain Development and Character Formation.47

Discipline...................................................................53

CHAPTER 7  The Apprenticeship of Being Human...............56

Small..........................................................................57

Slow...........................................................................57

Simple .......................................................................58

Solution......................................................................59

CHAPTER 8  The Virtue Argument ....................................62

Dignity & Responsibility.............................................63

Courage & Character Formation ..................................64

The Irony of Social Manipulation ...............................65

Moral, Economic and Virtue Arguments......................65

CHAPTER 9  Apprenticeship: Examples and Exceptions .......68

A Double Example: Geoffrey Canada & The Baby College..........68

An International Example: Parents as Teachers .............70

Exception That Proves the Rule: Roland G. Fryer .......71

CHAPTER 10  Truly Social Justice .....................................73

Society Level: Policy Makers & Advocates ...................74

Community Level: Educators ......................................75

Family Level: Parents .................................................77

Love Your Neighbor ...................................................79

APPENDIX 1  Underlying Classism? ..................................83

APPENDIX 2  The Practice of Parenting .............................88

Step 1: Reflection ......................................................90

Step 2: Resolve ..........................................................96

Step 3: Repetition......................................................100

APPENDIX 3: Recommended Reading.....................................103

AFTERWORD.....................................................................104

Three Nobel Prizes................................................................104

Muhammad Yunus' Three R's ................................................104

Al Gore's Inconvenient Truth ...............................................104

What Courageous Innovation Is Needed Now?.........................105

ABOUT THE AUTHOR.......................................................107

ENDNOTES........................................................................108

# The Apprenticeship of Being Human

## INTRODUCTION

As I walked home from my first day of teaching third grade, I couldn't get the words out of my head: "I am a failure." I had never failed before. In competitions, I hadn't always taken home first prize; but I had never failed. I had graduated at the top of my high school class, and had placed among the top 6 in pole vault in my home state for four consecutive years. College was more challenging, but I stayed on the dean's list every semester and graduated *summa cum laude* with a degree in philosophy. After graduation, I had enjoyed recognition in an internal consulting team at a global wealth management firm, and had opportunities to step into a "fast track" leadership development program at the firm.

In 2002, I resigned from the financial services to serve in a failing school in my neighborhood of East Flatbush, Brooklyn as a New York City Teaching Fellow. Eager to prevent educational failure, I now tasted first-hand the failure that was all too familiar to my students. I had nine weeks of graduate school under my belt to prepare me to teach. Yet on day one I had already failed. The students could see that I was "green," and an eight-year-old girl had already out-maneuvered me and undermined my authority. From what I had already learned in the first courses of my master's degree, I knew that failure on day one meant a long, hard year ahead.

My first class was comprised of thirty-two students ranging in age from seven to eleven, two-thirds of whom had not met the grade two year-end performance expectations. In the first week of school, I sat down to read one-on-one with Ari[1]. I knew from looking at his second grade report card that he was behind, so I picked out an easy reader for him. I asked him to begin reading. He looked at me sweetly, but puzzled. I pointed to the word "hi" on the page and asked, "Can you read me this word?" He shook his head. I asked, "Do you know those two letters?" He correctly identified them. Then I asked, "Do you know what they say together?" Again he answered, "No." As his teacher, *I* was expected to bring him to meet or

---

[1] All student names have been changed.

exceed third grade performance measures by the end of the school year. It was going to be a long, hard year indeed.

During the first week of school, I showed my class list to another third grade teacher. She looked truly shocked. "They gave you Karl?!" After two years in the second grade, Karl already had a school-wide reputation in a building that housed nearly 1,700 students spanning pre-kindergarten to eighth grade. Another teacher who had taught at the school for about twenty-five years cautioned me. She said, "I had a student like Karl once. He went on to murder a teacher." Already, by third grade, Karl was on a trajectory toward delinquency, and perhaps even felony.

There were two or three Aris in the class, who were two to three years delayed, and five or six Karls, who were emotionally disturbed. But there were also quiet children like Nicole. At the beginning of third grade she was only a year behind, but was quiet and courteous, and didn't attract any attention to herself – which is perhaps why she hadn't received more help to catch up. There were also bright children like Elisa and Cynthia. Elisa had strong reading and writing skills, asked excellent questions, and was able to focus on a task without being attended. Midway through the year, she and her mom lost their apartment and moved temporarily to a shelter in the Bronx. Elisa commuted well over an hour each way to school on the subway – and continued to learn and grow. Cynthia was already reading and writing fluently in both English and Spanish when she entered third grade. Her parents consistently encouraged and challenged her – even as they engaged in the process of learning English themselves. From this diverse, interesting, challenging group of students I was poised to learn.

## Questions, Questions, Questions

As a newcomer to education, I quite naturally began asking questions. Some of my questions were psychological in nature:

- Why were there so many emotionally disturbed students not receiving counseling, therapy, or some sort of help?
- What was their home life?

Other questions focused on issues of sociology:

- How much does early home life of children (the years before they begin schooling) matter for later achievement?

- How did the obvious culture gap between home and school affect communication, collaboration, and learning?

Some of my questions were clearly educational:

- What role did parents and caregivers play in the academic performance of students?
- How could children be three years delayed by third grade?!
- If it was already this bad by third grade, when did the achievement gap first emerge?

Since my wife was training at a medical school in the neighborhood where I taught, I inevitably asked public health questions:

- Why does there appear to be such an overlap among parenting, educational failure, and chronic health issues like obesity and diabetes?
- What common factors of early nurture affect health *and* education?

Finally, there was an economic set of questions:

- What role did my students' economic status have on their learning?
- What factors enable some children in poverty to learn, thrive, and escape from poverty?

These became my multi-disciplinary research questions, which I explored over the next nine years informally through teaching, parenting, parent engagement, educational entrepreneurship, and community participation; and more formally in the world of published educational and economic research.

The questions of early childhood parenting became even more personal and pressing when I became a father. After three years in the same elementary school, I took a child care leave to be full-time father to my daughter, who was at that time eighteen months old. I quickly discovered that despite having a master's degree in early childhood education, I had yet to learn what to expect and what to do with an eighteen-month-old. If that was true of me, despite my educational and social privilege, what must it be like for the parents of my students, many of whom had received neither positive modeling of parenting nor formal education in child development?

The questions that I was engaging were deeply personal, not only because I was a father and an educator, but because, for the majority of my adult life, I have lived in communities of poverty. For me, it is not an abstract question:

13

*How do we fix those people?* Rather, given the baseline brokenness within which *we* live, what are the most critical factors influencing responsible learning, social contribution and flourishing communities? The questions are not merely for the various academies of psychology, social science, education, public health, and economics. The question was, and is: *How do I love my neighbor as myself?* How can I seek for the children of others – my neighbors – that which I seek for my own children?

In asking this question, I am not merely adding ethics as another discipline in a multi-disciplinary inquiry. Rather, I am saying that this is personal because I'm talking about real people, not just statistics or trends. In the pages to come, I will argue that stories shape us. So it is appropriate at this point to state clearly that I have been (and am being) shaped by the Christian Story. The question, "How do I love my neighbor as myself?" does not arise in a vacuum. It is part of the Story of a community, of which I am a member. It is equally important to avoid the common mistaken assumption that people of different Stories cannot learn from and agree with one another. I trust that my discussion of the power of stories will demonstrate both the centrality of the question of how we love our neighbors *and* the importance of listening to and learning from people who are shaped by different Stories.[2]

## The Gap

As I began digging into the professional literature, it became increasingly clear to me that the achievement gap (the difference in performance between children of different cultural groups) is not the only gap. There was and is a gap between the research community and the primary stakeholders in education. Researchers write for one another (which is why peer review is an essential element of the academy), and for the stakeholders in their given field. In education, some of the most important research is directed to policy makers and educators, but rarely is it written for the most influential stakeholders: parents.

---

[2] In chapter 4, *Scripted: The Role of Stories*, I will differentiate between capital-S Stories, which animate our lives, and lower-case-s stories, which are particular stories like *The Billy Goats Gruff*.

This book is an attempt to bridge that gap, to present the most important implications of the contemporary educational and economic research to a broad audience in order to quicken educational and social renewal. Parents are, therefore, at the center of my target audience because they are the *chief culture architects* of their families. This little book offers parents a simple metaphor to understand the dynamics of early childhood, and focuses intently on:

1.  Four key areas of early child development:
    - Character
    - Competence
    - Creativity
    - Collaboration
2.  Three significant environmental factors in healthy development:
    - Love
    - Language
    - Literature
3.  Three keys to developing a nurturing home environment:
    - Reflection
    - Resolve
    - Repetition

Parents are also the core of my target audience because of the nature of human influence. Influence increases with nearness of relationship, durability of relationship, and level of responsibility. Consequently, each person has the greatest influence within his or her own household. Some people, such as a principal or city council member, *also* have significant influence at the community level. Still fewer, such as the United States Secretary of Education, have influence at a societal level. Since *every* person exerts tremendous influence within their closest and most durable relationships, I am deliberately addressing each group within their sphere of influence, small or large.

However, parents are not my only intended audience. All parents live within a community composed of people who *can* support or hinder their role; family, friends, neighbors, educators, and doctors top the list. Those communities exist in a broader society of individuals and institutions who can empower or disempower parents, including (but certainly not limited to) policy makers, administrators, and lobbyists.

So I have deliberately avoided writing a "parenting book." You may not have children, or be remotely interested in educational research. However, *everyone* is a neighbor and has neighbors. There is no one who is not a part of the web of relationships that compose neighborhoods, communities, and society. Consequently no one is untouched by the dynamics of early childhood parenting *and* no one is entirely without influence. Rather, as the subtitle of the book states, this is *Why Early Childhood Parenting Matters to Everyone.* Unpacking why early childhood parenting matters and what each sphere of influence can do is the task of this book.

For the many courageous individuals and organizations who already understand and embody this conviction, *The Apprenticeship of Being Human* is a simple explanation for non-experts of why what they do is so important to the fabric of society. I want the Early Intervention Specialist and Parent Educator to be able to hand this little book to a friend and say, *"This* is why I get out of bed every morning passionate about what I do."[3] I want ridiculously talented parents who have stepped away from lucrative careers to invest in their children as full-time parents to be able to say, "This is why what I'm doing is not foolish, but truly serves my children, our community, and society." I want economists like Art Rolnick, former Director of Research at the Federal Reserve Bank of Minneapolis, and philanthropists like J.B. Pritzker, founder of New World Ventures and president of the Pritzker Foundation, to be able to say, *"This* is why I invest so much of my time, passion, and wealth in early childhood initiatives." It is a book about parenting, but not just for parents.

My aim is to change the way we think in order to catalyze change in action at every level: family, community and society. Carter G. Woodson, considered the father of Black History, boldly declared, "If you can control a

---

[3] This is a deliberately "little" book. Much more could helpfully be said on the subject than I attempt in these pages. My purpose here is a 'manifesto,' a terse (and hopefully memorable) presentation of the importance of early childhood parenting, with a simple call to action.

man's thinking, you don't have to worry about his actions. If you can determine what a man thinks you do not have worry about what he will do." I am convinced that changing (not controlling!) the way we think about early childhood parenting on a societal, community and family level can have a profound effect on our daily practices, and therefore on the health of our families, communities and society. Furthermore, the heart of my argument is that in the earliest years of life, parents (or those who act in their stead) "control" their children's thinking by establishing boundaries and providing opportunities for their children. Indeed, children are apprentices to their parents as they learn to participate in the craft that we call human culture.

In my own experience, there is no escape from this claim. My children imitate me and my wife – sometimes to our embarrassment. Likewise, the parents of my students had a singular effect on their children, for good or for ill. For example, my student Mitch wasn't raised by his mom. She was strung out on drugs, and he bore the marks of in utero drug abuse. Mitch's grandmother adopted him and took an active stake in his education. She told me up front that Mitch was a crack baby, but that she wasn't going to let that ruin his life. If he had any trouble academically or socially, she wanted me to put a note in his homework folder that very day so that she could know and address it. Mitch had a lot against him as a black boy, developmentally affected by his mom's drug habit, abandoned by both his parents, and stuck in a large class of struggling students. Yet he had one thing going for him: a grandmother-turned-mother who loved him deeply and was unwaveringly committed to him. The good news for Mitch is that despite all of the challenges in his life, loving parental involvement is the single best predictor of any child's educational achievement. To celebrate, cultivate, and inspire that loving involvement in parents, foster parents, adoptive parents, caregivers and those who surround them is the aim of this little book.

So it is appropriate at this point to thank and honor my wife, Rebecca. She is the embodiment of loving, nurturing commitment to our children. Throughout her medical training as a developmental pediatrician, there was never any question that our children came before her vocation. Our daughters see in her that meaningful vocational and social contribution, vital and important as they are, are secondary to the enormous influence she exerts in her most primary relationships in our family. It is my hope that this book will inspire other parents to recognize the unparalleled influence they have on their children, particularly in the earliest years of life.

As I look back on my own childhood, I am deeply grateful for my own parents. In particular, I am thankful for the ways that they sowed stories into our family life. I remember my mother reading volumes aloud in the car as we took road trips that could span seven states in two days. I recall our morning routine of breakfast, reading, and prayer which shaped the way that I experience the world. Our lively conversations around the dinner table each evening have embedded in me a desire to cultivate that kind of lively family culture. These are, among others, the things that I remember, and now attempt to imitate. Yet I am aware that there is far more, below the surface, that I do not consciously recall, which is just as important in forming my habits and loves. For all of this love, I am grateful.

I am indebted to many wise parents (and at least one astute not-yet-parent) who took time to read and critique this book before its publication. Noah Blumenthal, whose books are well worth reading, saved me from writing a book that no one would read. Keith Zafren, founder of the Great Dads Project, directed me in the rudiments of rhetoric. Chris Upham exercised his talents as an analytic philosopher in helping me to avoid philosophical gaffes. Chris Esposito Bernard, Sandy Davis, Jeff Burkett, Cindy Mahlberg, James Marroquin, Daniel Bartholomew, Alex Forrester, and my father, Greg Scharf, all offered valuable critique at various stages in the writing process. They have helped me in refining the content of the book, addressing my audience, and learning the art of rhetoric. It is my hope that this book will at least in some measure honor their help and wisdom.

# CHAPTER 1

# Apprenticeship

Every morning when I leave my home in Harlem, I pick up trash that others have thrown on the sidewalk and in the flowers that my seven-year-old daughter, Elisabeth, planted with me. On one of these occasions, my daughter asked me, "Daddy, why do people throw their trash in front of our house?" After some reflection, I answered, "Because their parents didn't teach them not to."

Is it really that simple? Am I just oversimplifying in order to provide an answer that my seven-year-old can understand? Consider another example: One day on the bus, we watched a girl about nine years of age discard her half-eaten hot dog on the floor of the city bus. Her mother said nothing. Her silence spoke volumes in condoning her child's behavior. In his book, *Culture Making*, Andy Crouch describes the dynamic of how parents set the horizons of possibility for their children: "In one family's culture it is 'impossible' for people who love each other to argue with one another; in another family's culture it is 'impossible' for people who love each other *not* to argue with one another." Family culture has the power to communicate whether throwing your food on the floor is acceptable, or unacceptable. The initiation of a child into that family culture *is* apprenticeship.

There was a time when, in many cultures, apprenticeship was the primary mode of training in a craft or skill. Young people apprenticed themselves to masters (often their own parents), whether of a trade like ironwork, or an art like sculpting. Although apprenticeship is less prevalent today as a manner of formal vocational training, it remains the primary mechanism by which children learn to participate in human relationships, and affects virtually every aspect of personal and public life – including the flowerbed in front of my house and the city bus on which we travel.

Early childhood is the apprenticeship of being human. Like the apprenticeship of an artist, it is composed of both explicit instruction and ongoing interaction and imitation within personal relationships. Just as an apprentice in an art or trade learns techniques that are essential to the mastery of that art or trade, so children learn techniques of participation in the craft of human culture. However, the apprenticeship of being human is also a markedly different from the mastery of an art or trade in that the 'craft of life' spans all other crafts. Someone can know a particular craft (such as writing), do it well, and still be a rotten member of the human race. This is because to know how to make something or do some particular thing well is not the same as knowing how to live well in all aspects. The apprenticeship of being human is learning the 'craft of life.' It is the context in which we learn to acquire other skills, and how to use those skills well – or poorly.

The disproportionate influence of these early years lies in the fact that apprenticeship occurs constantly in children's most primary relationships during a period of unparalleled brain growth. Early experiences, in turn, have a lifelong impact on a child's character, competence, creativity, health and ability to collaborate. Consequently, this is not a parenting book that encourages parents to employ a novel or effective technique. Rather, it is an exploration of the dynamics of human development and their implications for nurturing virtuous children and flourishing societies. The question is not whether we will embrace a particular parenting method, but whether we will recognize that we are already mentors with little apprentices watching and learning from our every word and action. Then, with that recognition, we can wield our influence wisely and well.

The dynamics of apprenticeship are, perhaps, most evident in the acquisition of language. If you venture to a kindergarten classroom in Staten Island, one of the first things you are likely to notice (unless you're a Staten Islander) is the dialect of the children. Although it is just a twenty-five minute ferry ride from Manhattan, this island has its own distinct accent and dialect. Why? Children in Staten Island are just like children everywhere else: they acquire language in the context of their most primary relationships as an essential part of learning to speak. It is learned in part by direct instruction, "It is pronounced *this* way . . .", but the vast majority is learned implicitly and continually by interaction and imitation. The acquisition of accent and dialect in early childhood is the language dimension of apprenticeship. It happens to everyone, everywhere; it can't be avoided.[4] In much the same way, claiming that early childhood doesn't establish a child's horizons of possibility is like a Staten Islander claiming, "I don't have an accent!"

---

[4] My argument is that parenting matters in ALL levels and sectors of society, not just among the poor. Indeed, in Appendix 1 *Underlying Classism?* I argue that those who think that parenting just matters for the poor are naïve and classist.

CHAPTER 2

## What's the Big Deal?

*"Existing [educational achievement] gaps
impose the economic equivalent of a permanent national recession—
one substantially larger than the deep recession the country is currently experiencing."*
(McKinsey & Company, 2009)

## The Education Crisis

The United States faces an unprecedented educational crisis. Fewer than 7 out of 10 students graduate from high school nationally – and in some communities fewer than half complete high school.[i] That means that if you go to the grocery store or the gas station, you have a roughly one in three chance of getting a young person to ring you up who has not demonstrated the perseverance and skill to complete high school. Of those who do graduate, the American College Test (ACT) estimates that only 25% of 2011 high school graduates taking the ACT had the appropriate skills needed to succeed in college.[ii] This crisis is not evenly socially distributed; there exists a large and alarming achievement gap among various cultural groups, which manifests in social, economic and ethnic stratification. Consequently, an overwhelming proportion of students – disproportionately represented by some cultural groups – are unprepared to take an active, responsible role in civil society.

For employers, there is a rapidly dwindling pool of talent from which to draw. For citizens and residents of this country, it suggests that an enormous proportion, if not the majority of our citizens-in-training, will not be able to creatively and courageously meet the economic, environmental, social and political crises of our day. They may not even be equipped to give you the proper change if you pay for your groceries with cash.

The education crisis is not "news." Everyone in the educational community accepts that there is a deep problem with our educational outcomes. I merely want to impress the reader at the outset with the depth of the problem and how early it begins. I will then suggest why the enormous effort and resources devoted to addressing the crisis have yielded such meager results. With few exceptions, educators and policy-makers have been trying to close the achievement gap from within the formal education system; I am going to argue that this will be fruitless until the 'parenting gap' is also closed.

## The Parenting Gap

In education, the problem is not that *all* children are failing to meet age-appropriate learning goals; some students continue to thrive, learn and grow. The problem is that there is a chasm between these two groups – the failing and the thriving – which is frequently called the *achievement gap*. All significant educational reform efforts struggle to understand and address this gap.

When does the achievement gap emerge? Educational failure starts early; in fact, it starts long before school begins. The achievement gap between disparate social groups,[5] measured in verbal, emotional and cognitive ability, is significant by 3 years of age.[iii] The social dimension of disadvantage makes it an extremely sensitive subject. However, the social entrepreneur who has been one of the most successful in preventing and addressing the achievement gap has been most courageous and forthright about the social

---

[5] Throughout this book I use the phrase "social groups" and "cultural groups" deliberately and meaningfully because the attributes that these groups have in common are primarily social and cultural, not racial or economic. In some cases these social and cultural lines overlap with racial and economic lines, but that does not mean that race or class are the key factors. Indeed to treat race and class as primary (rather than secondary or tertiary) treads the soil of racism and classism.

origins of the gap. Paul Tough explains in his outstanding book *Whatever it Takes: Geoffrey Canada's Quest to Change Harlem and America*:

> Geoffrey Canada [founder of the Harlem Children's Zone], for his part, understands why so many social scientists and black activists are reluctant to identify parenting as a cause of the racial achievement gap. But in Harlem, he believes, the simple reality is that most of the neighborhood's poor, black parents are not adequately preparing their infants and children to be educated. And to him, the practical advantages of addressing that fact overshadows the political costs.[iv]

What Goeffrey Canada has understood is that it is not the skin color of his constituency that constitutes disadvantage. What happens in the home in the earliest years of life is the proper measure of advantage or disadvantage, because parent involvement is the single best predictor of a child's educational achievement.[v] Beneath the achievement gap, there lies a parenting gap.

## The Fathering Gap

What happens in the home in the earliest years of life is significantly shaped by *who* is in the home in those years. At present, 27% of all children under 19 live apart from their fathers. Like the parenting gap, the fathering gap is not evenly distributed across social groups. "Forty percent of fathers who didn't finish high school are not residing with their children, a living situation shared by only 7% of fathers who graduated college."[vi] In other words, the very kids who need the most support at home are vastly less likely to have that support.

The consequences are as obvious as they are tragic. Children from father-absent homes are five times more likely to live in poverty. "In 2002, 7.8 percent of children in married-couple families were living in poverty, compared to 38.4 percent of children in female-householder families."[vii] Children from father-absent homes are more likely to use and abuse drugs – even after controlling for other social and environmental factors.[viii] They are also at dramatically higher risk for neglect: "Compared to living with both parents, living in a single-parent home doubles the risk that a child will suffer physical, emotional, or educational neglect."[ix] Father absence is a risk factor for health: "Marital disruption after birth is associated with a 6-fold increase in the likelihood a children will require an emergency room visit and 5-fold increase of an asthma-related emergency."[x] In school, fatherless children are twice as likely repeat a grade,[xi] and twice as likely as their peers from two-parent homes to drop out altogether.[xii]

In a 2011 Father's Day *Time Magazine* article entitled *The Fathering Gap: The Pitfalls of Modern Fatherhood*, Belinda Luscombe surveys the tragic disparities of father involvement and concludes: "The wealthy and well-educated and their children are reaping the benefits of more engaged fatherhood much more than those who struggle, creating a spiral of income inequality that will be harder and harder to reverse." Income inequality drives relational inequality; and vice versa. That is the fathering gap.

## Toward a Tipping Point

Malcolm Gladwell's *New York Times* bestseller *The Tipping Point: How Little Things Can Make a Big Difference* examines social epidemics through a critical lens: Why is it that some ideas, products and movements (some good and some decidedly harmful) have the epidemic quality of spreading rapidly? Gladwell contends that social epidemics are heavily dependent on individuals with specific and unique social gifts. He highlights three:

1. *Connectors* – those who connect the right people to make things happen
2. *Mavens* – those who find and disseminate important information
3. *Salesmen* – those who have persuasion and charisma to move others to action

These people – connectors, mavens, and salesmen – draw an idea, movement, or product to a tipping point: the place where it becomes a social epidemic. Gladwell explains:

> The word 'Tipping Point,' for example, comes from the world of epidemiology. It's the name given to that moment in an epidemic when a virus reaches critical mass. It's the boiling point. It's the moment on the graph when the line starts to shoot straight upwards. . . . Wouldn't it be cool to try and look for Tipping Points in business, or in social policy, or in advertising or in any number of other nonmedical areas?

The purpose of this book is to inform mavens, and provide a simple manifesto for connectors and salesmen to precipitate a *Tipping Point* in which communities embrace and fulfill the single most powerful role in establishing and maintaining a just and flourishing society: being a parent.

# Chapter 3

## Brain Building: Birth to 5

*"If babies' bodies grew at the same rapid pace as their brains, they would weigh 170 pounds by one month of age."*

Early Childhood Colorado

There are three common objections to the claim of a parenting gap, each of which must be answered.

**There is no parenting gap.**

**The educational system can overcome the parenting gap.**

**The parenting gap is simply a difference in parenting style.**

The first objection disappears quickly in light of the vast disparities in school readiness which will be highlighted in this chapter. The second objection is more substantial, and even noble in raising the bar for educators to meet the challenges presented. However, an examination of the nature and rate of brain development demonstrates that if not impossible, such remediation of early deficits is nearly impossible. The third objection is the most substantial. What are the grounds for advancing a particular understanding of, or approach to parenting? Doesn't it come down to parental preference? The answer to this objection is two-fold. The first answer is empirical: parenting significantly affects educational, social and developmental outcomes. The second answer is qualitative, and centers on how parents influence their children's norms. Indeed, the answer to this objection is so important that chapters five, six and eight are devoted to the primacy of virtue, and the parental role of nurturing character.

## Parents Can Cause Brain Damage

In 2008, researchers at the University of California Berkeley found detectable differences between children from low-income families and children from higher-income families in the response of the prefrontal cortex, the part of the brain that is critical for language use, problem solving and creativity. "Kids from lower socioeconomic levels show brain physiology patterns similar to someone who actually had damage in the frontal lobe as an adult," said Robert Knight, director of the Institute and a UC Berkeley Professor of Psychology. Silvia Bunge, UC Berkeley Assistant Professor of Psychology reflected, "The study is suggestive and a little bit frightening that environmental conditions have such a strong impact on brain development." The researchers' conclusion was shockingly simple. Study co-author W. Thomas Boyce summarized:

> In work that we and others have done, it really looks like something as simple and easily done as talking to your kids can boost prefrontal cortex performance. . . . [C]hanging developmental outcomes might involve something as accessible as helping parents to understand that it is important that kids sit down to dinner with their parents, and that over the course of that dinner it would be good for there to be a conversation . . . [xiii]

The recommendations make clear that while the study segmented the target population by income, it is nurture that is the critical resource.

Why are these early years so vital? One significant part of the answer lies in the nature and rate of brain development. The human brain grows from 25% to 80% of its adult volume between birth and age three. If a child grew in stature at the same rate, the average American boy would be four feet seven inches by his third birthday. And since the brain grows to 90% of its adult volume by age 5, this prototypical American boy would be five feet two and a half inches at his fifth birthday.[xiv] Furthermore, *Zero to Three*, a research and advocacy organization, summarizes:

> [B]rain development is 'activity-dependent,' meaning that the
> electrical activity in every circuit—sensory, motor, emotional, [and]

cognitive – shapes the way that circuit gets put together. . . . Every experience--whether it is seeing one's first rainbow, riding a bicycle, reading a book — sharing a joke — excites certain neural circuits and leaves others inactive. Those that are consistently turned on over time will be strengthened, while those that are rarely excited may be dropped away. Or, as neuroscientists sometimes say, "Cells that fire together, wire together."

The following graph shows how facets of brain development overlap, and why early experiences are so critical. New synapses are constantly and rapidly forming *in response to stimuli*. Each experience then has a cascading effect on subsequent brain development.

Human Brain Development
Synapse Formation Dependent on Early Experiences

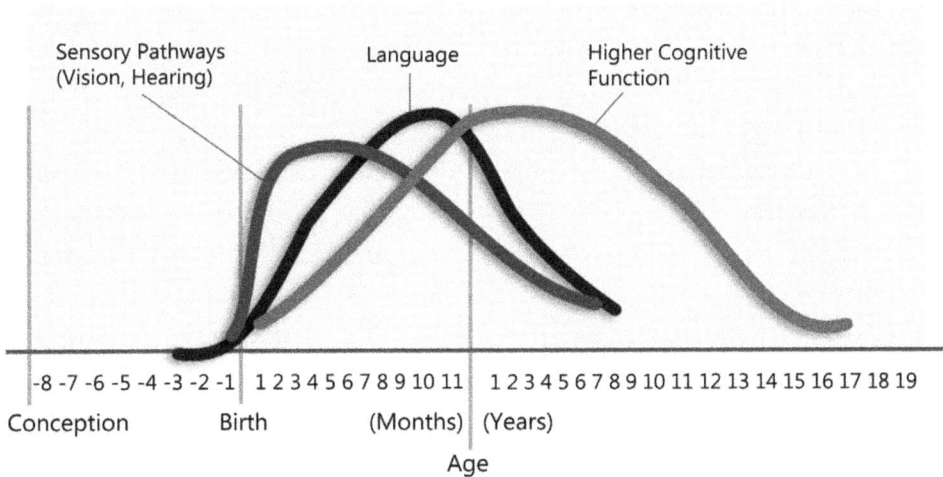

Source: Nelson (2000)
National Center for Children in Poverty,
Improving the Odds for YOung Children, 2008

Early experiences shape the physical structure of a child's brain and can have lifelong effects.

If the headline reads, "Parents can cause brain damage," the bottom line reads, "The best way to prevent brain damage may be to have regular, meaningful conversation."

## Normal & Normative

In addition to the rate and sensitivity of brain development, a child's early experiences establish his sense of what is *normal* and *normative*. If a young child is accustomed to watching television for two hours a day (like the average American child under age 6), she will inevitably have a different sense of normal – and different brain development – from the child who spends hours a day looking at books. Likewise, a child who enjoys a serving of vegetables at mealtime and snacks on fresh or dried fruit will have a different experience of normal from the child who is accustomed to eating fast food for dinner, and a bag of chips and a can of soda for snack. Or consider bedtime routines: the three-year-old who has a repeated, predictable experience of brushing her teeth, reading books with a parent and going to bed at 7:30 each night will have different expectations from her age-mate who stays up every night until eleven o'clock and crashes without having brushed her teeth. The lifelong impact of these repeated "normal" experiences on a child's language acquisition, social skills, nutritional and oral health, and sleep habits are difficult to overstate.

Routines are easy to see because they are repeated patterns of action, of things that we do. Ask any three-year-old, "What do you do to get ready for bed?" and she can recite the routine. Yet inexperience (what does *not* happen) is just as powerful as experience – though less recognizable – in establishing a child's sense of normal. Father absence is the most powerful example of this. For a young child in a father-absent home, *not* spending time with dad is normal; *not* having a male authority figure and role model may be normal; *not* forming emotional bonds with a man may be normal. As a male early childhood teacher, I experienced my students' inexperience vividly. Many of my students had never had a positive relationship with a man that had lasted as long as the school year. Their early experiences of normal made walking into my second grade classroom a completely *abnormal* and bewildering experience for them.

Just as repeated experience – and inexperience – in every area of life shape a child's experience of *normal*, so those experiences also shape an understanding of *normative* – what is good and valuable, and what is wrong and unacceptable. Do parents spend time daily in dialogue with their children? Do families regularly spend time together enjoying and discussing shared experiences such as reading a book, playing a game, going for a walk, or creating art? What families repeatedly do communicates what is valuable and profoundly influences what a child loves. In much the same way, parental interaction establishes what is not acceptable. If a child interrupts a conversation, how do parents respond? Do they patiently correct, with clear direction of how to politely say, "Excuse me"? Or do they ignore the child until she tantrums? Or do they berate her? Or hit her? Parents' repeated responses to inappropriate behavior establish norms both in *what* they prohibit, and in *how* they respond to inappropriate behavior. Remember the girl who threw her hotdog on the floor of the bus? It didn't happen in a vacuum.

## Practice Makes (Almost) Permanent

Mastering any skill requires diligent practice. Is there any exceptional athlete, musician, actor, scientist, scholar, teacher, writer, orator or artist who does not invest countless hours in focused, thoughtful practice? If this is the path to excellence in virtually every field of skill and knowledge, is it not fair to assume that this, too, is the path to excellence for children in learning how to learn, and in learning how to participate responsibly in society? And if repeating a bad habit – as simple as how you hold a pencil – only makes it more difficult for a person to break, does it not stand to reason that repeated practice can be the path to mediocrity or failure on the same principle that makes the achievement of excellence possible?

Looking at practice through the lens of apprenticeship helps to avoid missing the forest for the trees. Since children imitate their parents in the 'craft of life,' parents influence not only what and how children practice, but how they pursue the craft of life. Amy Chua made headlines with *Battle Hymn of a Tiger Mother* not because she provided structure and practice time for her children to become outstanding musicians, but because she threatened to donate her seven-year-old daughter's beloved dollhouse to the Salvation Army if she couldn't play an admittedly difficult piano piece perfectly by the next day. What is at stake is not merely excellence, mediocrity, or failure in a particular skill, but the practice and cultivation of virtue and honor in how we treat other human beings.

In the ensuing chapters, I will argue that the cultivation of virtue is more important and more valuable than excellence in any particular field of learning or performance. The apprenticeship metaphor is not a veiled attempt to impose a bourgeois vision of family life onto others, but a lens through which to examine parenting beliefs and practices – including bourgeois values.

## Repetition

We are what we repeatedly do. Even if parents give no thought to the art of parenting, children learn by experience a way of being in the world. Their experience of *normal* in the early years naturally and inevitably becomes the standard by which they judge all other experience. Perhaps the most poignant example is the family meal. Does a family eat together on a regular basis? If so, what happens? Do they watch television together? Or do they have a conversation? Do they listen to one another, or is everyone talking at once? Are they constantly distracted by handheld devices? Around this table, or this television (as the case may be), children learn how to interact with other people through repeated experiences. If someone objects that watching television together isn't interaction, and doesn't teach interaction, that person has missed the central point that we learn from repeated experience *whatever* it is. If the family rarely or never eats together, the repeated experience of *not* eating together establishes an entrenched pattern. Any repeated experience, whatever it is, establishes a child's sense of *norms* and *normal*. For some, the focal point of interaction may be a screen, instead of another person; or it may be that family members interact with others only through screens. This will have significant repercussions for learning to relate – or not relate – to others.

## Resolve

Every human being makes purposeful decisions. We *choose* one thing instead of another every day, and these choices have consequences. For example, parents can *choose* to read with their children, or choose to put them in front of a screen. This choice has significant consequences for a child in learning to be human. In the context of a shared book, a child learns to communicate by interpreting words, gestures and body language from the reader, and expressing himself in words (if he is old enough to speak), and through his own gestures and body language.

In addition to learning to interact with others, he is being initiated into a way of being in the world. If reading a book together happens only rarely, the impact is not nearly so great as if it is repeated; hence the primacy of repetition. Each communicates something about the value of literature, words, and interpersonal communication; resolved repetition shows that we deliberately cherish something. We can choose to repeatedly act in ways that demonstrate what we love.

## Reflection

Socrates famously stated, "The unexamined life is not worth living." As human beings, we have the capacity to reflect on the relative value of different activities and resolve to make repeated change. This power of reflection is vividly evident in the practice of athletes. It is possible by the force of great resolve and faithful repetition to train for a marathon. The person who sets a running schedule – and adheres to it – can prepare for a race she has never run in her life. And yet, if she does not reflect on her training, her resolved repetition may only serve to establish bad habits. Great runners reflect on their stride. Are they running on their heels? Are they altering their gait as they descend hills? This discipline of reflection is essential to learning to run *well*. In a similar way, parents invariably teach and influence their children by the force of repetition. By resolve they can choose to practice certain activities, such as reading together or a family meal. Yet in the absence of reflection, they may simply ingrain habits of choosing poorly-written books, or arguing and interrupting one another at the dinner table.

Reflective parenting is the discipline of asking difficult questions. My repeated actions represent what I value. But do they embody what I want to value? Where do I need to break out of a rut, or establish a new routine that will be good for my family? One of the most valuable questions for parents to ask is whether a particular approach to parenting achieves its desired outcome. Some parents, desiring their children to clearly understand right and wrong, are harsh in correcting an inappropriate action. Their intentions are quite honorable: they want kids who know and choose what is right. But their actions, sadly, can have quite the opposite effect. If a mother yells,

"Don't lie to me!" does it promote honest confession and repentance? If the same mother calmly but firmly asks, "Is that the truth?" will the child be more or less likely to admit his fault and choose to speak truthfully next time? The resolve may be identical. Reflective resolve, used repeatedly, will produce a decidedly different outcome.

If you think of these three elements like gears, reflection is the key gear because it turns (shapes and influences) resolve. Resolution turns repetition by establishing routines and rhythms of life that embody what we desire to communicate. Repetition exerts its own force like a wheel rolling down a hill whether or not there is any reflection or resolve. Reflection and resolve can point the wheel to keep it on the road – and keep it from flying off the cliff.

# CHAPTER 4

## Scripted: The Role of Stories

*"I can only answer the question 'What am I to do?' if I can answer the prior question 'Of what story or stories do I find myself a part?'"*

Alasdair MacIntyre, *After Virtue*

If reflection is the critical gear in changed action, stories are perhaps the ideal locus of reflection. Like the force of repetition in shaping the experiences of a child, so Story plays a central role, regardless of the degree to which parents deliberately and reflectively embrace a particular Story. We are continually hearing stories – from books, on television, in movies, on stage, in theater, and through the news.[6] Perhaps the most recognizable capital-S Story is the one that we commonly call *The American Dream*. In broad strokes, first expressed by James Truslow Adams in 1931, it states that citizens of every rank feel that they can achieve a "better, richer, and happier life." This Story gives shape to the lives of vast swaths of immigrants to, and citizens of, the United States. The Story guides our decisions in where we choose to live, the books we select to read (and those we deliberately omit), the educational paradigms we adopt for our children, the kinds of vocations

---

[6] Does the medium through which story comes to us matter? In my discussion of *Literature* in Chapter 6, I tackle this important question.

we pursue, and the diligence with which we ply our trades. In short, the Story of which we are a part guides our actions and decisions. It is precisely because Story is so central to who we are and how we make sense of the world that reflection is so valuable and vital.

## Indwelling

The living out of a Story, whether the American Dream, or the struggle for civil rights, or any other guiding Story, is what I would call *indwelling*. We live in it. We allow it to shape us. Sometimes we are conscious of, and grateful for (or perhaps even resentful of), the influence the Story has on our lives; we may even repeat it like a mantra. But in daily life, these Stories more often function like lenses. They are not that *at which* we look, but that *through which* we look, thereby influencing the way we perceive and respond to and even create the realities around us. Or, to change the metaphor, we indwell a Story like a surgeon indwells a scalpel. The adept surgeon does not focus on the instrument in his hand, but the scalpel functions as an extension of his hand; he indwells it, and is attentive to what it touches, not the thing itself.[7]

Not only is every child born into the Story of a family and community; each child also becomes a character in a living Story, and thus *indwells* the story – as Ruby Bridges did from an early age in the struggle for civil rights. Ruby Bridges, as one of the first black children "integrated" into a white school in New Orleans in 1960 is not an exception, but an example.

When Ruby began attending the William Frantz Elementary School, all of the white families refused to send their children to school. Instead, many gathered outside the school to revile and even threaten six-year-old Ruby. They were so virulent that President Kennedy ordered federal marshals to escort Ruby into the school every day. Yet Ruby never responded to the mobs. In Robert Coles' picture book *The Story of Ruby Bridges*, he narrates an amazing encounter, which is worth quoting at length:

> Then one morning, something happened. Miss Hurley [Ruby's teacher] stood by a window in her classroom as she usually did, watching Ruby walk toward the school. Suddenly, Ruby stopped –

---

[7] I owe the idea of a surgeon indwelling a scalpel to Lesslie Newbigin. Indeed, I have deliberately 'apprenticed' myself to Newbigin in learning to think about thinking, and his fingerprints are all over my writing.

right in front of the mob of howling and screaming people. She stood there facing all those men and women. She seemed to be talking to them.

Miss Hurley saw Ruby's lips moving and wondered what Ruby could be saying.

The crowd seemed ready to kill her.

The marshals were frightened. They tried to persuade Ruby to move along. They tried to hurry her into the school, but Ruby wouldn't budge.

Then Ruby stopped talking and walked into the school.

When she went into the classroom, Miss Hurley asked her what had happened. Miss Hurley told Ruby that she'd been watching and that she was surprised when Ruby stopped and talked with the people in the mob.

Ruby became irritated.

"I didn't stop and talk with them," she said.

"Ruby, I saw you talking," Miss Hurley said. "I saw your lips moving."

"I wasn't talking," said Ruby. "I was praying for them."

Every morning, Ruby had stopped a few blocks away from school to say a prayer for the people who hated her. This morning she forgot until she was already in the middle of the angry mob.

Ruby did not have the privileges of wealth. Her father was a janitor, and her mother cared for the children during the day and scrubbed floors in a bank at night. In Ruby's own words, "We were very poor, very, very poor." In these hard circumstances, Ruby was initiated into the Story of a family and community that taught her to love her enemies, to pray for those who mistreated her, and to do good to those who hated her. This is the Story which shaped her actions as an unlikely, yet meaningful, actor in American history.

Her white peers at William Frantz Elementary school, whose parents not only withdrew them from the school, but also came to the school to mock, threaten and berate six-year-old Ruby were no less born into the Story of their families and communities. They, too, *indwelt* and participated in a Story as active characters in human history. The Story that parents indwell, and

37

into which they initiate and indoctrinate their children, has the power to shape the history of a nation – even through the actions of a six-year-old girl.

## Initiation

Early childhood is the *initiation* of a child into a way of being in the world. A child's early experiences teach him how to navigate the social context into which he was born. Unlike "hazing" as an initiation into a fraternity, the initiation of early childhood may or may not be intentional and is not confined to Greek Week. For example, Martin Luther King Jr. was well prepared by family nurture to recognize and address the injustices of his time. He received from his parents a Story that makes sense of the world, and guides meaningful action. He was, in a very real sense, apprenticed to his parents and initiated into ways of addressing injustice with words and courage rather than violence. Dr. King is not the exception; *every* child is initiated into the Story of a family and community.

## Indoctrination

The process of initiation is also one of *indoctrination*, not in the pejorative sense of brainwashing, but in the old, historic definition: "to instruct especially in the fundamentals or rudiments," or, more simply, "to teach." In the earliest years, children learn the fundamentals of how to be human. For example, in these years they learn how to participate in conversation. One child has a parent who makes eye contact, listens carefully, asks clarifying questions, and gives genuine affirmation. Another child is accustomed to being ignored by his parent, or "talked down to," and frequently observes and experiences belittling and hostility. Both children are being indoctrinated in the fundamentals of human communication and relationship – and as a result will relate very differently with others.

In this way, children's lives are "scripted." Their families and communities provide the script of the Story into which they are initiated. That Story, in turn, guides the pursuit and development of character.

# CHAPTER 5

## Clever Devils: Why Virtue Trumps Test Scores

*"Education without values, as useful as it is,*
*seems rather to make man a more clever devil."*

C.S. Lewis

We live in an age in which the success of education is often measured entirely on children's performance on tests. In such a time, it is wise to ask if this is the proper measure of education. Would we, for example, be satisfied if all the children in a particular school or city exceeded the performance benchmarks for their respective ages – only to foster increased consumption, indolence and careless disregard for the environment? Or what if they devoted their intellectual prowess to design more potent and destructive landmines? Or what if they developed more efficient and clandestine methods of human trafficking? Clearly, competence in skills alone is not a sufficient measure of education – or early nurture. What then are the proper measures of education and early nurture over which parents have such tremendous influence?

## Character

The most significant role of early nurture and formal education which follows later is to form the character of children. How people treat one another is the very foundation of a just society – the kind of place in which the following three traits (competence, creativity, and collaboration) flourish. Without the baseline of a just society – which begins in a just family – competence, creativity and collaboration can be used in ways that destroy communities rather than build them. When parents cherish and cultivate the virtue of their children, their children love learning, and communities flourish.

In the cultivation of character, there is no escape from the centrality of humility. An eager, life-long learner has a deep personal understanding of how much learning remains ahead. To receive correction and reproof that are essential for mastery of any skill, humility is paramount. In learning to exercise creativity well, one must be willing to fail repeatedly – a process which both requires and teaches humility. Humility enables a person to work well with others through authentic listening. And it is only one example of virtue that affects the acquisition of skills and the formation of healthy relationships.

In my first year of teaching, I used a card system for "classroom management." At the front of the classroom I hung a large posterboard. On it, each child had a small pocket with 3 cards: one red, one green, and one yellow. Every child started with the same color exposed (green, for instance). If and when I needed to address a student's inappropriate behavior, I would "change the card" to the second color (yellow, for example). A second major infraction would change it to red. The idea is that it helps children *see* that their behavior has consequences.

On one occasion when I was meeting my students in the school yard after lunch, I saw one girl, Felisha, push another student. I told her that when we returned to the classroom I would change her card for inappropriate behavior. By the time we reached the classroom, my mind was on teaching, and I forgot to change her card. As we began our math lesson, Felisha raised her hand. I called on her. She said, "Mr. Scharf, you forgot to change my card."

I stopped the math lesson. I turned to the rest of the class, "Do you see what Felisha just did? She took responsibility for her actions. I had forgotten about what I said, and she easily could have 'gotten away with it.' But she reminded me. Do you know what that tells me? It means Felisha has integrity. Felisha is exactly the kind of student I want to have; and if I was an employer, I'd hire her in a heartbeat because I know that she can be trusted." The point is not that Felisha didn't make mistakes. (She had just pushed her classmate!) Her humility enabled her to admit the wrong that she had done to her classmate and take responsibility for her actions. Her character didn't just influence her own self-discipline in learning; it influenced our whole classroom culture in having integrity and taking responsibility for our actions.

## Competence

After virtue, competence is paramount to the flourishing of individuals, relationships and communities. In fact, character and competence cannot be separated. Being competent means knowing how to perform an activity well, and consistently performing it well. Competence is an important component of character: a person cannot be virtuous without demonstrating hard work, integrity, and persistence – qualities that begin to form around age 1 when a child can begin to learn to put his toys away. Indeed the early development of these character traits and learning skills set a child's life-long trajectory for learning. Learning begets learning, and motivation begets motivation. Competence develops confidence, which breeds excellence.

It isn't enough simply to be a "nice person." In the work place, the sheepish statement, "Well, he's a nice guy," is often code for, "He's easy to get along with, but incompetent to do the work that he's supposed to do." Contributing to a community – in a family, school, neighborhood or society – entails cultivating competence. The accolade, "You sir, are a gentleman and a scholar," has become a cultural expression precisely because *both* are important.

## Creativity

Competence and creativity, too, are intertwined. To be competent in anything implies creativity and problem solving. This includes creative expression like music, painting, drawing, sculpting, baking and sewing; it also entails the ability to use the resources at hand to accomplish a given task. In a home where creativity and innovation are intentionally cherished, children solve problems in new ways and develop life-long patterns of innovation. *Every* child will experience conflict and disagreement; learning early to develop creative solutions – and observing parents who creatively and consistently resolve conflict – prepares a child to embrace and solve problems. Guided by virtue, human creativity solves problems and creates beautiful artifacts that enables human flourishing (and prevents a lot of temper tantrums).

Consider the example of Majora Carter. As an African American woman in the South Bronx, she was surrounded by problems: pollution, joblessness, noise, and lack of access to green space. Where many people see only problems, Majora saw a creative solution. She founded Sustainable South Bronx to help address all of those problems. Through Sustainable South Bronx's *Smart Roof LLC*, local residents install structure, soil, and plants on the roofs of existing buildings. What are the benefits? The roofs improve energy efficiency of the buildings, absorb carbon dioxide, and absorb sound. Importantly, Smart Roof employees become stakeholders in their own neighborhoods, and stewards of the local resources. This experience in "green" entrepreneurship immerses the team in creative community problem-solving, a skill that team members can pass on to their children so that they have the tools to tackle the problems around them.

## Collaboration

A team is more than the sum of its parts; and children learn to work in teams (with parents and siblings!) from their earliest years. One of the most important skills that young children learn on a soccer team is how to pass; and the difference between a great soccer team (of any age) and an immature one is quickly evident in whether the players run like a flock of sheep in pursuit of the ball, or spread out and pass frequently and skillfully. On and off the field, the ability to collaborate is nurtured through practice in the context of real relationships, and is part of the very fabric of life.

Learning to build a supportive, collaborative environment is one of the most important responsibilities of any leader – the owner of a small business, the principal of a school, or the manager of a restaurant. How do those leaders learn to nurture a collaborative environment? Like all of us, they learn by experience. Those who have many experiences of a vibrant, collaborative team will most naturally be able to build that sort of team because they have practiced the art of collaboration – by apprenticeship. Leaders who have little experience of positive collaboration are at a distinct disadvantage in building the kind of culture that is essential to a flourishing team.

Families are no different. Parents learn by experience how to create a collaborative family culture in which everyone contributes and everyone is valued. Those parents who have experienced a collaborative family environment will be best prepared to nurture that environment in their own families. *Together* families that are marked by character, competence and creativity create the kind of environment where *everyone* wants to be.

The formation of virtue in human persons and justice in human relationships is of primary importance. If a family, community, or society prizes competence above character, it will multiply clever devils. If it prizes creativity above virtue, it will have no firm grasp on goodness, truth and beauty by which a cultural creation can be judged good or destructive. If it celebrates collaboration above character, it sows and cultivates the seeds of its own destruction. Of course, this is a paraphrase of Mahatma Gandhi's famous dictum: "The Roots of Violence: Wealth without work, pleasure without conscience, knowledge without character, commerce without morality, science without humanity, worship without sacrifice, politics without principles." If we are deaf to his wisdom, we may well attain a root of violence: knowledge without character.

# CHAPTER 6

## Cultivating Character

*"What is the proper measure of disadvantage?*
*Is it poverty?*
*Measures of childhood home life?*
*Evidence suggests quality of parenting is key.*
*Parenting is the scarce resource.*
*Disadvantage is not always closely linked to family income or even parental education . . .*
*The real measure of child poverty is the quality of parenting.*
*Not necessarily financial distress."*

James Heckman, *Return on Investment: Costs vs. Benefits*

Parenting is the measure of poverty. But parents are not the only ones who have influence in parenting. This chapter addresses the dynamics of the home that define advantage and disadvantage, and identifies practical ways that parents can provide a rich home environment regardless of economic status. These insights are just as valuable for those who surround and support parents as for parents themselves. Parents are *always* acting within the fabric of a community and society that can affirm and strengthen, or disempower and disable them.

## Routines & Rudiments

The true measure of a child's privilege or disadvantage is the love and nurture they receive from their parents, which is profoundly influenced by their own cultural inheritance from parents and grandparents. My claim is simply this: that *all* children are indoctrinated from the time of their birth into a Story that gives shape and meaning to the shared life of their family and community in the context of a larger society. They are taught, often more implicitly than explicitly, the *rudiments* of being human through their daily *routines* in the context of their most primary relationships. These routines, by the force of repetition, establish a child's sense of what is normal and what is normative.

The interrelation of routines and rudiments is most vivid in the use of words and books. Consider this staggering statistic:

> By one estimate the typical middle-class child enters first grade with 1,000 to 1,700 hours of one-on-one picture book reading, whereas a child from a low-income family averages just 25 hours.[xv]

One child experiences routines that celebrate children's books, a practice that expands his horizons, his vocabulary, and his capacity to understand others. He experiences the joy of well-chosen words as *normal*. By contrast, another child finds the experience of a picture book decidedly *abnormal*. Yet, as Nobel Prize winning economist James Heckman constantly reminds us, "[T]he real measure of child poverty is the quality of parenting." A parent who has limited education or cannot read *can still* tell rich stories and establish routines that profoundly teach the rudiments of being human.

## Poverty of Language

Why is there this shocking correlation between poverty and language? Andy Crouch makes a striking connection. He says, "To be poor is to be unable to 'make something of the world.'" Words are the "tools" of exploration and creation. Not having many words, or not knowing how to use them well, has a crippling social and economic effect. Gladys Hunt, writing for parents on the power of language and literature, connects wealth and poverty of language:

> The right word in the right place is a magnificent gift. Somehow a limited, poverty-stricken vocabulary works toward equally limited use of ideas and imagination. On the other hand, the provocative use of the right words, of a growing vocabulary, gives us adequate material

with which to clothe our thoughts and leads to a richer world of expression.[xvi]

The judicious, creative use of words *is* a language-rich environment, and can exist in *any* family, regardless of ethnic, economic, or social status. Yet poverty of language is a key predictor of why some poor remain poor; they lack the tools to make something of the world. It should be no surprise that children born into these families acquire the family vocabulary which, tragically, "works toward an equally limited use of ideas and imagination" with which to break the cycles of poverty.

The enjoyment of a language rich home is certainly not only found in the homes of the wealthy. Take for example Laura Ingalls Wilder, the author of the *Little House on the Prairie* series. By contemporary measures Laura was "at-risk" and "poor" in almost every way. She moved frequently across harsh territory, without food security. She needed to work diligently in the home in order to help her family provide for their basic needs – from cultivating, preserving and preparing food, to making and mending clothing. Living in the cold northern plains, she often had only one pair of shoes (and well-worn hand-me-downs at that) in which to trudge frozen roads to a one-room school house where even paper was a luxury. Yet she had loving parents who nurtured a capacity for storytelling that has enriched every subsequent generation with her frontier memoirs. Laura Ingalls Wilder deserves not our pity, but our emulation in diligence of work and celebration of words. From her we can, perhaps, learn to measure the well-being of a child in terms of a loving, language-rich environment.

## Practice & Perseverance

If you ever have the privilege of seeing and hearing Yo-Yo Ma perform Bach's *Cello Suites*, your jaw will drop with the sheer beauty of the experience. Many a child who has seen such a performance has walked away saying, "I want to be able to do that!" and wise parents have replied, "You, too, can learn to play beautifully with lots and lots of practice." Whether it is watching a graceful dancer or an extraordinary wood carver, or a superlative musician, children can learn early the connection between excellence and diligent practice.

How many people have been able to play a Bach concerto the first time they sat at a piano? How many people have ridden a unicycle on their first attempt? Is there a single Olympic athlete who does not engage in resolved, reflective practice of her skill? Virtually every skill depends on *opportunity* and *practice*.

Parents, then, wield enormous influence in the nurture of their children by providing opportunities to try new age-appropriate activities, and establishing routines for them to practice the most important skills. When parents consider their children's development to be *their* responsibility to nurture, providing these opportunities is both natural and fun.

With respect to education and early nurture, there is no substitute for practice and perseverance for two reasons. The first is obvious: a child won't master any desired skill, from participating in respectful conversation to riding a bicycle, without persevering practice. The second is no less important: The disciplines of practice and perseverance in early childhood develop lifelong patterns. A child will understand implicitly that learning can be hard work, that it requires diligence in doing the things that we don't necessarily feel like doing at the time, but that it is the natural, normal, and only way to mastery. It is the way that Yo-Yo Ma became one of the greatest cellists in history.

## The Hothouse of Brain Development and Character Formation

In the home environment, there are three factors over which parents have influence that significantly affect brain development: love, language, and literature. These conditions form the 'hothouse of development.' Like the seedling in a greenhouse, a child who has consistent affirmation and encouragement, coupled with respectful, creative use of language has the ideal conditions for brain development – and therefore for the cultivation of character, competence, creativity and collaboration. By contrast, the child who experiences harsh relationships and a poverty-stricken vocabulary is like a seed dropped in the wilderness.

## Love

The acquisition of new skills always involves risk-taking. The famous developmental psychologist, Lev Vgotsky, calls this period of learning the *zone of proximal development*, commonly abbreviated ZPD. The ZPD refers to

47

tasks that are too difficult for a child to master independently, but which can be learned with assistance.

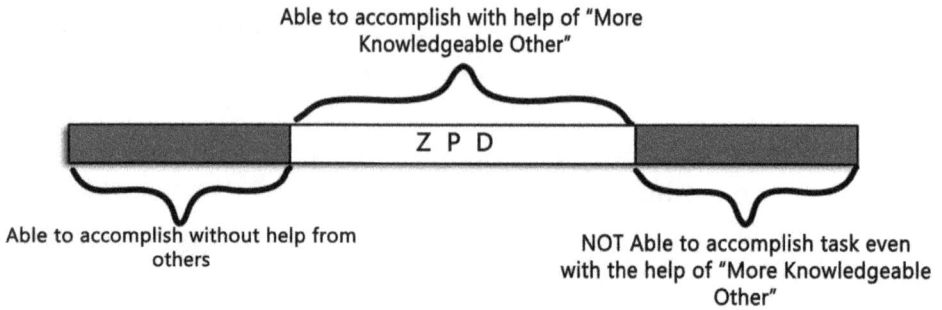

Able to accomplish with help of "More Knowledgeable Other"

Z P D

Able to accomplish without help from others

NOT Able to accomplish task even with the help of "More Knowledgeable Other"

(Image: Peter Rich, 2007)

Vgotsky's thesis, which is relatively simple, is that appropriate support fosters healthy development. Conversely, if a child *lacks* affirmation and support – or worse yet, is actively discouraged – then she will be less likely to take risks in the ZPD and acquire new skills. The consequence is a vicious feedback loop. Not only is the child who is discouraged by her parents not taking appropriate risks, she also feels the shame and stigma of not progressing, which in many cases makes a child even less willing to take what would otherwise be appropriate risks.

Now consider the opposite end of the spectrum. I walk into a playground where a mother is teaching her son to climb on the jungle gym. With *each* step, she says, "Well done! You can do it! That's right! Keep going! Now the other foot!" The affirmation and affection that she expresses toward her child in the most common of circumstances keeps him nearly constantly in the ZPD. This child is *always* trying something new, testing the limits of his abilities – and breaking them.

In contrast to the negative feedback loop, the child with the affirming parent experiences a positive loop. With each new skill, he builds confidence; with each affirmation, he is emboldened to take new risks. In James Heckman's concise summary:

> Life cycle skill formation is dynamic in nature. Skill begets skill;
> motivation begets motivation. Motivation cross-fosters skill, and skill
> cross-fosters motivation. If a child is not motivated to learn and
> engage early on in life, the more likely it is that when the child
> becomes an adult, he or she will fail in social and economic life.[xvii]

Consequently, early advantages accumulate, and so do early disadvantages.

The confidence that a child builds in receiving love is not what is commonly called self-confidence. It is, more properly, "love-confidence" which is the foundation of proper confidence, healthy interdependence, and genuine humility. In receiving the unconditioned love of a parent, a child gains the security that her acceptance does not depend on her performance - or even on her character. Love creates humility that can truly, joyfully and freely love others. The beloved child is gloriously free from the insecurity of performance - and is therefore free to develop skills, abilities and passions.

## Language

This dynamic of love and language in the home manifests itself in the sheer number of words spoken, and the tone of communication. In one study conducted by Betty Hart and Todd Risley at the University of Kansas, they estimated that children from professional (i.e. white collar) families would hear, by age three, about 30 million words. Their counterparts from families on welfare would hear only 10 million words by the same age. The number of encouragements and discouragements children heard by age three was just as different: "By age three, the average professional child would hear about 500,000 encouragements and 80,000 discouragements. For children on welfare, the ratio was reversed: they would hear, on average, about 80,000 encouragements and 200,000 discouragements."[xviii] Not surprisingly, the children's vocabularies reflected their families: children of professional parents had vocabularies of about 1,100 words at age three, while children from welfare families spoke only about 525 words.

| At age 3 | | |
|---|---|---|
| | Children of Professionals | Children of Parents on Welfare |
| **Words Heard** | 30 million | 10 million |
| **Encouragements** | 500,000 | 80,000 |
| **Discouragements** | 80,000 | 200,000 |
| **Words Spoken** | 1,100 | 525 |

# Ratios of Affirmation & Prohibition

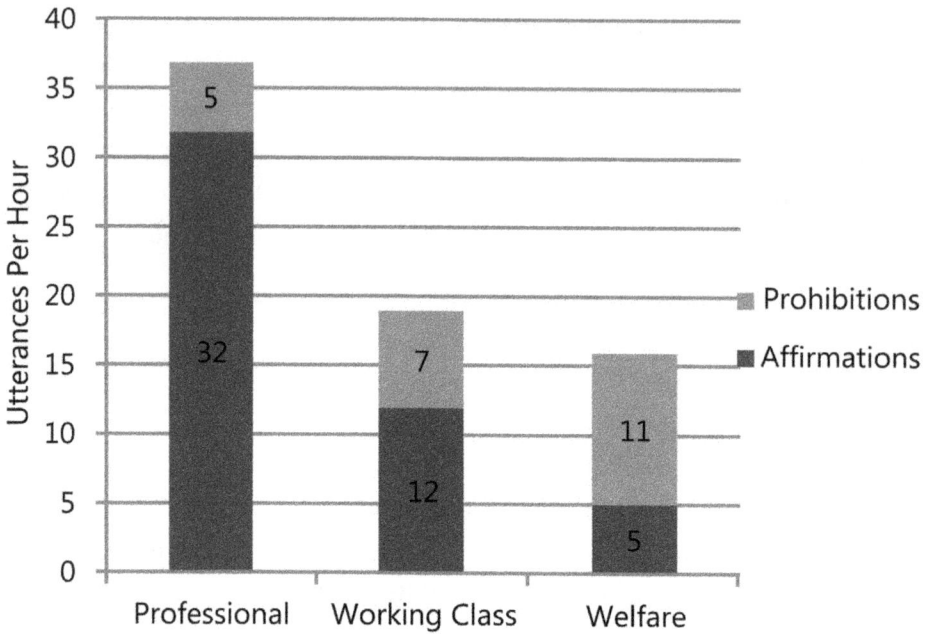

Hart and Risley summarized their findings in these words:

> Cognitively, experience is sequential: Experiences in infancy establish habits of seeking, noticing, and incorporating new and more complex experiences, as well as schemas for categorizing and thinking about experiences. Neurologically, infancy is a critical period because cortical development is influenced by the amount of central nervous system activity stimulated by experience. Behaviorally, infancy is a unique time of helplessness when nearly all of children's experience is mediated by adults in one-to-one interactions permeated with affect. Once children become independent and can speak for themselves, they gain access to more opportunities for experience. But the amount and diversity of children's past experience influences which new opportunities for experience they notice and choose.[xix]

And that is precisely why the American Academy of Pediatrics recommends no television at all for children under two years of age.

Words, well used by loving parents, can foster healthy, exuberant acquisition of language. By contrast, words used to discourage and denigrate have the effect of stunting linguistic and emotional development, which obviously has wide-reaching repercussions on a child's success later in life.

## Literature

Just as love provides the stimulus for appropriate risk-taking, words form the tools with which children explore the world into which they are born. It is for this reason that literature and poetry play such an important role, as in this poem:

> When Mother reads aloud, I long
> For noble deeds to do -
> To help the right, redress the wrong;
> It seems so easy to be strong,
> So simple to be true.
> Oh, thick and fast the visions crowd
> My eyes, when Mother reads aloud[xx].

A constantly growing breadth of vocabulary provides a child the tools with which to explore the world around him – to name things, to question, and to enjoy. The child with 525 words at age 3 has fewer than half of the exploration tools of the one with 1100 words at the same age. Dr. Seuss – a master of using few words well – used those few words to extol a wide acquaintance with words:

> The more that you read, the more things you will know.
> The more that you learn, the more places you'll go.

The acquisition of language in the context of loving relationships is inseparable from the process of learning and exploring. Without a growing vocabulary and an imagination quickened by well-told (and well-illustrated) stories, there are but few paths children can tread.

Here I ought to admit that I am using "literature" to continue the alliteration of *love* and *language*. Yet what I have in mind is not limited to the written word. Rather I mean to include diverse means of engaging children with stories and beauty. It is possible for a parent to show affection, to encourage a broad vocabulary, and yet fail to expose their children to great stories. It is for this reason that I want to champion the importance of engaging children with beautiful stories in as many ways as possible. *Literature*, as I am using it here, includes picture books, novels, poetry, historical fiction, theater, film, oral storytelling, and yes, even television.

Among these media, there are some that foster flourishing human relationship better than others. The beauty of parents reading to and with their children is that the reading itself is a shared experience that encourages meaningful human interaction. At any time they can pause and discuss what happened. In like manner, they can pick up the story again in the park, on the train or bus, in the car, or at home. Likewise, oral storytelling has a striking personal dimension. A friend of mine, Jim, started inventing stories for his children as they traveled on vacation. It became part of their daily routine, and each night his girls would eagerly ask for the next "chapter" in his improvised narrative. Jim's own acquaintance with great stories furnished him with the ideas and words to tell enchanting stories to his children.

Television is at the bottom of the list because although it can form the context of a shared experience and tell a good story, it has two significant weaknesses. First, television doesn't move at the pace of the story-consumer. When reading a book or poem alone or with others, the reader can pause. The listener (or reader) can ask questions. The medium itself encourages thought and interaction. By contrast, television barrels on in a way that harms rather than helps reflection. Second, although technology is changing, television is usually interspersed with advertisements, the purpose of which is to incite us to want and purchase products or services. In short, the pauses in television are not for the purpose of reflection, discussion and authentic human interaction, but for enticing us to want something that we don't have. These two factors have led us as a family not to own a television. We can enjoy great stories through film, books, theater, and oral storytelling in ways that avoid these interruptions.

Literature is a mode of apprenticeship. We listen to, learn from, and imitate poets, historians, storytellers, playwrights, screenwriters and authors. When we find one who is masterful in his or her craft, we joyfully immerse ourselves – perhaps in the picture books of Kevin Henkes, or the playful stories of Beverly Cleary, or the poetry of Robert Louis Stevenson. In doing so, we observe and absorb rhythms of speech, manners of expression, and creativity of thought. Not only that, but we refine our taste for clarity of expression and masterful turn of phrase so that we recognize great literature by the experience of it, and not merely by being told, "This is great literature."

## Discipline

Parents are stewards of love, language and literature as they cultivate virtue in their children. Parents are also responsible for discipline. Discipline involves *reflectively* choosing to do what is good, and thereby forming good habits. However, much of life is *reflexive*. In many situations, we don't have the leisure to stop and think. A child throws a temper tantrum in the grocery store, and we must respond by reflex. And we do well or poorly based on the habits we have formed over time. The principle of routines and rudiments applies as much to us as parents as it does it does to our children.

Perhaps the best illustration of this is the batting cage. To become a great hitter in baseball, you go to the cages. You think about your swing, your stance, your shift of weight and rotation. You build up the nerve to stay in the batter's box even when you turn up the speed. You train your eyes and arms – your reflexes – to hit balls that are coming at you at a variety of speeds and heights. The point of all this is not to learn to hit in the cage. It's to achieve success in the game. You practice *reflectively* so that you can respond *reflexively* in a game situation, without having to think about it. If you haven't spent the time and energy in the batting cage, you may still (if you're lucky) get a hit in a game, occasionally. But you shouldn't expect to be able to hit consistently, because you haven't trained your reflexes.

The same is true of virtually every field of learning. How do you get comfortable driving a car at 120-150 miles per hour? You practice reflectively (on a closed track!) so that on race day your reflexes and instincts are well trained. How do you become a great chef? You train your fingers to move quickly and nimbly. You train your judgment to discern how much of a certain spice is going to add flavor to a meal without overpowering it. How do you become a great swimmer? You spend hours upon hours refining your strokes so that on the day of competition, swimming is second nature and you can pay attention to staying with, or ahead of, your competitors. How do you become a great cellist? You practice for hours on end until your fingers move like dancers on the strings so that you can attend not simply to the strings, or even merely to the musical score, but to the conductor.

The mastery of virtually any skill involves moving from conscious, disciplined thought to the ability to perform the skill reflexively and intuitively – by second nature. When you first learned to hold a fork, it was awkward and challenging. With time and practice it becomes second nature. You can carry on conversation and do many other things because you don't have to focus on holding your fork. The same is true of driving a car, typing on a computer keyboard, and every other repeated skill.

Parenting is like these other skills. When it is practiced reflectively, our reflexes improve and wise parenting becomes "second nature." Thinking that we can become great parents overnight is like thinking we can learn to hit home runs overnight. It's nonsense. We only become great parents over time, slowly, as we train ourselves, think deeply about it, analyze where we went wrong and make corrections. By deliberately practicing the strategies of good parenting, we form good habits and eventually develop good reflexes so we can achieve the success we desire in "game time" – those critical moments when we must respond by reflex.

On one occasion, we had a family join us for dinner in our apartment. Aria, the five year old, was disobedient and obstinate, deliberately throwing food on the floor, refusing to eat her food, and talking back to her parents. It was embarrassing for all of us, and painfully evident that our friends (her parents) had not established healthy reflexes. Instead, they had built patterns of "warning" Aria, which amounted to indulging her behavior. She knew that they hadn't developed the disciplines of healthy, firm, respectful confrontation. So, in "game time," eating dinner in the home of friends, they had no control of their child. She knew it and they knew it. Exasperated, my friend, Karl, turned to me during dinner and said, "Graham, will you discipline her? She listens to you, but she doesn't listen to me."

I could help re-establish order at that meal, but I couldn't break the long pattern of indiscipline with a single action. Aria listened to me because she knew that I meant what I said. She didn't listen to her parents because she knew that their threats were empty. When her father said to me (in front of her), "She doesn't listen to me," he was verbalizing and validating her expectations. To change those expectations is hard work. It takes discipline:

the self-discipline of reflection and planning in order to learn how to better respond to and discipline a child.

We can only expect to help our children form good character when we are leading them on the same path we've walked. We are helping them to form reflective habits of character so that they can respond reflexively in ways that are honorable, truthful, and loving. Discipline is a word that first applies to us as parents in cultivating habits of heart and action and then, secondarily, to that discipline which we impose (often reflexively) on our children with the hope that they will embrace our discipline, and it will become for them self-discipline.

# CHAPTER 7

# The Apprenticeship of Being Human

*"A basic unit of culture is the family, where we first begin making something of the world...
It can take us decades to appreciate all the ways in which the culture of our families set our
horizons of the possible and the impossible. Until we leave our families and venture into the
homes of our neighbors and friends, or perhaps the family home of a future spouse, we are
likely not even to realize all the ways that our family sets our horizons. . . .
Family is culture at its smallest - and its most powerful."*

Andy Crouch, *Culture Making: Recovering our Creative Calling*

Early childhood is the apprenticeship of being human. A child doesn't
have to be "taught" to be an apprentice; she *is* one. By interaction and
imitation, she learns to explore and make her way in the world. In her most
primary relationships, she acquires words – the tools of exploration and
understanding – and learns how to use them. Her early experiences, positive
and negative, establish her baseline of normal, the lenses through which she
will see the rest of her life. In the family, she is initiated into a Story of a
family and community. For better or for worse, the family is the studio in
which children begin the apprenticeship of being human.

Apprenticeship is not a "method" of parenting employed by some
"successful" parents; it is a description of what always happens in a child's
most primary relationships in the earliest years of life. If this dynamic is
understood and embraced, parents, neighbors, educators and policy makers
can make wise decisions in the home, community, schools, and government

that cultivate virtue and human flourishing. If the dynamics of apprenticeship are ignored or marginalized, we as citizens will continue to pay the social costs . . . equivalent to a permanent national recession.

## Small

In addressing problems on the scale of the achievement gap, which impose the economic equivalent of a permanent national recession, we are tempted to "think big." It would be wiser, and more effective in tackling such a tremendous problem, to deliberately "think small." We would do well to think about the influence that parents (or those who act in their stead) have in shaping the horizons of the possible and impossible for their children.

What is the most powerful form of structural oppression? It is the same structure that can be the most powerful force for the cultivation of virtue, wisdom, and excellence. It is the family. Family is culture at its smallest — and its most powerful. It is therefore the most powerful lever in affecting and influencing cultural and educational transformation.[8]

## Slow

As myriad diet marketing schemes demonstrate, human beings are suckers for speed. We want problems — and particularly big, painful problems — fixed now. Solutions that take time irk us. We assume that there must be a better, faster way. With respect to human development and character formation, there isn't a way to speed it up. Every child takes eighteen years to grow from birth to age eighteen. Educational calamity can't be repaired overnight.

There is, however, an enormous leverage to the earliest years of life because of the rapid rate of brain development. During the first five years of life a child's brain forms billions of neurons and hundreds of trillions of

---

[8] There is an obvious and important irony to this claim. In arguing for the importance of family culture, I am tacitly acknowledging the significant power of other cultural forces, particularly the institutions and policies that can empower or disempower families. Each entity of social organization, formal and informal, has its own sphere of influence and responsibility. My point is not that *only* one matters, but that *each* flourishes when it acknowledges and empowers the roles of the others.

connections, called synapses, among these neurons. If you compare the formation of neurons (which can be as rapid as 2 to 3 million *per second*) to webpages, and synapses to links on the internet (the most rapidly growing technology in human history), it is like racing a Ferrari against a tricycle. The internet can't keep up with the infant.

Brain development in early childhood is breathtakingly fast, and every experience not only influences how a child interprets later experiences, it affects the very physical structure of the brain. Consequently, investing time, energy, and focus on the earliest years of a child's life has a magnified effect for the rest of his or her life.

## Simple

Addressing the educational achievement gap doesn't require a complex solution.[9] The solution, though difficult to implement, is relatively simple in nature, and can be seen in the following three questions:

> What is the most powerful unit of human culture?
> What is the period of most rapid brain development?
> What is the single best predictor of a child's educational achievement?

The family is the most powerful unit of culture, and exercises its greatest influence during the rapid brain development of the earliest years of life. Further, parent involvement is the single best predictor of a child's educational achievement, and significantly affects life-long health and social contribution. James Heckman's diagram on the following page paints the picture of return on investment (ROI):

---

[9]There is an obvious parallel here to physical health. What are the two most important levers of physical health? Diet and exercise. The prescription is simple; the immense challenge is helping people to form healthy habits of diet and exercise.

## Figure 1: Rates of Return to Human Capital Investment at Different Ages: *Return to an Extra Dollar at Various Ages*

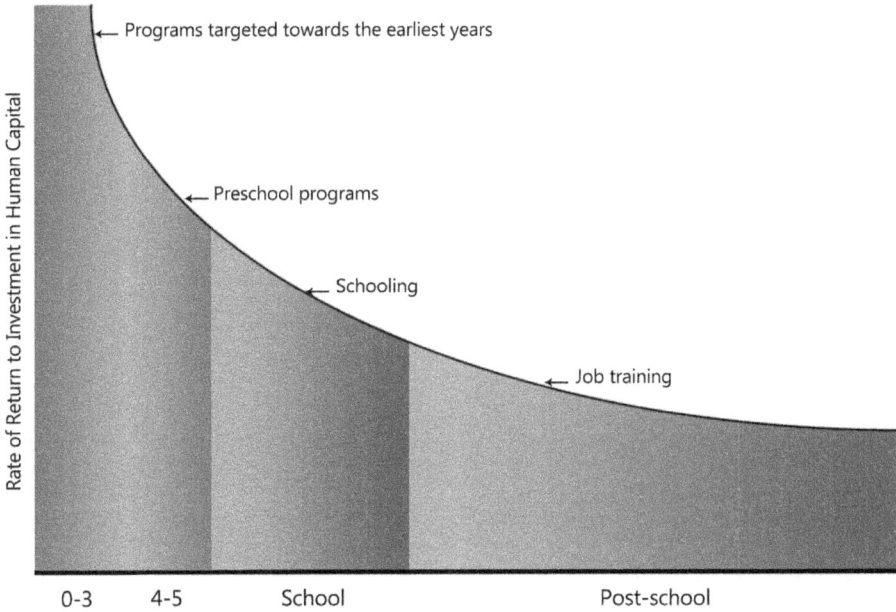

Source: Heckman (2008).

Why is the return on investment curve shaped like this? Early childhood *is* the apprenticeship of being human. In the earliest years we learn how to learn; we learn how to relate to others and the world around us; we develop a posture toward virtue, inquiry and creativity. We acquire words, the tools of exploration and creation, and practice using them to understand, navigate and make something of the world.

## Solution

To say that any one course of action would "solve" the educational crisis would be a dramatic and laughable oversimplification. There are indisputable labor issues, funding disparities, and myriad other interconnected challenges. The point is not to down-play any of these areas in which reform is genuinely

59

needed; it is rather to ask a simple question: In a world where resources (time, energy, and money) are limited, which investments pay the biggest dividends?

Over the past forty years, the federal government has tripled per-pupil spending on K-12 education (after adjusting for inflation), and real, cumulative per-pupil (inflation-adjusted) local, state and federal spending has more than doubled in the same period; yet reading scores and high school graduation rates remain relatively flat.

## The "Link" Between Education Spending and Student Performance

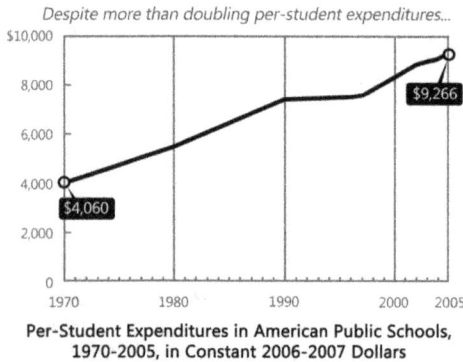

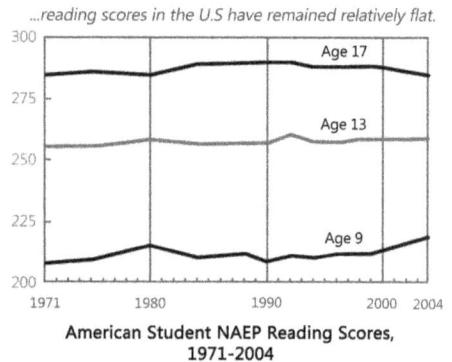

*Despite more than doubling per-student expenditures...*

*...reading scores in the U.S have remained relatively flat.*

**Per-Student Expenditures in American Public Schools, 1970-2005, in Constant 2006-2007 Dollars**

**American Student NAEP Reading Scores, 1971-2004**

Sources: U.S. Department of Education, National Center for Education Statistics, National Assessment of Educational Progress, "National Trends in Reading by Average Scale Scores." updated July 6, 2005 at *http://nces.ed.gov/nationsreportcard/ltt/results2004/nat-reading-scalescore.asp* (April 14, 2008). and *Digest of Education Statistics: 2007*, Table 174, at *http://nces.ed.gov/programs/digest/d07/tables/dt07_174.asp* (August 19, 2008).

Chart 4 · B 2179 ☎ heritage.org

By contrast, James Heckman reports:

> Early interventions promote schooling, reduce crime, foster workforce productivity, promote adult health through several channels and reduce teenage pregnancy. It can redistribute resources with a fixed budget and improve child and social welfare. These interventions are estimated to have high benefit-cost ratios and rates of return, in the range of 6–10% per annum compared to the post-war return to equity of 5.8%.[xxi]

In economic terms, James Heckman has demonstrated that there is no question. Not only does early investment far outstrip increased K-12 spending, it exceeds the average equity ROI since WWII. Money – family, community, and societal money – is best invested on family support in the earliest years of life. That is the compelling economic argument for early investment.

However, that is not *my* argument. It is a good one, and James Heckman has championed it heroically. My thesis is that there is a virtue argument for early investment even stronger than the economic argument. A child's brain development and character formation are inextricably intertwined, as the repeated experiences of early childhood establish a child's sense of normal and normative. Early childhood is the apprenticeship of being human. It is precisely *because* early childhood functions as the apprenticeship of being human that the economic argument works.

# CHAPTER 8

## The Virtue Argument

*"Virtue is a good habit consonant with our nature."*
*St. Augustine*

A vibrant, prosperous economy is a good thing *if and only if* it is the result of, and in service of, a just and equitable social order. Pursuing prosperity for its own sake can, and will, lead to injustice and inequity. Therefore, as strong as the economic argument for early investment is, it is and must be secondary to the virtue argument. A just society is not merely a place where just laws are equitably enforced; it is a society in which citizens cherish, practice, and cultivate positive virtue. Lesslie Newbigin brilliantly summarizes St. Augustine's monumental *City of God* on the connection between a flourishing family and a vibrant society:

> Love creates order first in the family and among neighbors, and then, by extension, in the city and the nation. Without this, even the earthly commonwealth cannot exist. It is love that creates justice.[xxii]

A just society begins in a just family with loving nurture. Love quickens latent abilities that would not otherwise develop. If virtue is cherished and cultivated in the family during the most sensitive and critical period of development, its members will be prepared to grow and flourish in civic responsibility. Virtue is the durable foundation of prosperity. Conversely, in the famous words of Dr. Martin Luther King, "Injustice anywhere is a threat to justice everywhere." Indeed, injustice in the smallest and most powerful unit of human culture – the family – is a threat to neighbors, city, and nation.

## Dignity & Responsibility

How do wise teachers deal with "bad" kids in an elementary classroom? Give them responsibilities. Designate them the line leaders, or make them responsible for wiping the board. It is vastly more effective than punishment. Why does it work so well? One would think that the "bad" kids are the ones who would be least able to handle responsibility. Yet giving appropriate responsibility works because responsibility and dignity are intertwined. Giving a child responsibility communicates that he is important to the class, the community of learners. (Most of the "good" kids have already internalized this message. They know that their contributions to the class are important.) With responsibility, a child's experience of dignity as a real and important person soars.

Dignity and responsibility are not only intertwined for children; they are interrelated for everyone, including parents. Marian Wright Edelman, the founder of the *Children's Defense Fund* has boldly stated:

> Parents are their children's most important teachers and mentors, and they bear primary responsibility for nurturing their sons and daughters while keeping them safe. Yet parenting is one of the most undervalued and least prepared for roles in America.[xxiii]

In addressing the needs and failures of parents who are not fulfilling this responsibility, it is essential not to unintentionally undermine the dignity of these parents by transferring parental responsibilities to "experts" or programs. Rather, like the "bad" kids in the classroom, it is possible – and essential – to communicate to parents that *they are their children's most important teachers, mentors, role models, coaches and cheerleaders* and to support them in fulfilling this responsibility. When these parents feel the dignity and weight of their responsibility – and receive appropriate support – they rise to the challenge.

Over the past several years, I have had the privilege of watching parents rise to the challenge. Tyron was one of those surprising parents. I couldn't help but notice that there was another father taking his daughter to and from pre-kindergarten every day on the city bus that we rode to school. Not only did we ride the same bus, but we did the same things. We read books with our girls, laughed together, and talked about the school day. If someone else saw the two of us, they would immediately notice all the differences: I'm white; he's black. By clothing, you'd guess that I came from the Upper West Side, and he from Harlem. How did we, who were so obviously different, share the same parenting practices? My curiosity got the best of me, and I introduced myself as we got off the bus one day. Tyron told me that a few years ago he had been looking for work, and had gotten a job as a teacher's aide in the school our daughters attended. In that role, he experienced firsthand the importance of education and the influence of parents. Although he now worked for an uptown record label, he not only made sure that his daughter was in a good school, he also *invested* time, love and energy in their relationship during their thirty minute bus ride. Tyron felt the dignity and weight of his responsibility as a parent – and rose to the challenge.

## Courage & Character Formation

No one would suggest that an abandoned single mother who works diligently to raise four boys in the South Bronx is not courageous. The difficulty of her situation is the index of her courage. Indeed, if an action is not difficult, it is, by definition, not courageous. Courage is performing good and wise action *despite* difficulty, pain, opposition or risk.

If this is true, then the parents who have the most stacked against them can show the greatest courage and virtue in responsible and wise parenting. A parent who has never observed a healthy marriage, or experienced a loving relationship with a parent, or participated in a supportive educational atmosphere, and yet takes a small step of turning off the TV to read with her child demonstrates enormous courage! The reason that we celebrate those who rise out of poverty to serve others is precisely because it is so difficult for them to do. To break the cycles of single parenting, of delinquency, and of irresponsibility takes herculean effort. Those who do it should be truly honored for their courage.

I have claimed with James Heckman that the proper measure of disadvantage is the quality of parenting. If, therefore, a parent experienced this sort of disadvantage as a child, any and every effort that he or she makes to *be* a good parent is a valiant act that should be honored and celebrated.

For children learning to read there exists what is sometimes called the Matthew Effect, referring to Jesus' teaching in the Gospel of Matthew: "Whoever has will be given more" and its corollary – "whoever does not have, even what he has will be taken away" (Matt. 13:13 and 25:29). In short, early readers become better readers, which is why early language experiences in the home matter so much. However, in parenting it should be noted that there is also the Great Reversal of Jesus' teaching: "But many who are first will be last, and the last first" (Mark 10:31). Those who have experienced the disadvantages of fractured homes and poverty of language and yet seek to nurture their children with love, language, and literature are far more virtuous than those who, having experienced the privilege of such a childhood take little care to nurture in their children a love for virtue and wisdom. The difficulty of their situation is the index of their courage – and virtue.

## The Irony of Social Manipulation

If we recognize that the dignity of parents is proportional to the responsibility accorded them, then well-intended policy decisions that seek to shift parental responsibilities to social service organizations, schools, and elsewhere *will* as a result erode the dignity of the very families that they seek to serve. And since these parents are the ones who can show the greatest courage and honor in overcoming the disadvantages they have experienced, programs and policies that engage in a sort of "parent replacement therapy" may succeed in improving the test scores of disadvantaged children in the short-term, at the expense of their parents' dignity and the fabric of their community. This is the irony of social manipulation: it accords to the manipulators the dignity and responsibility which is denied to the recipients of their "benevolent" action.

## Moral, Economic and Virtue Arguments

There are three forceful arguments for the critical role of early childhood parenting. The moral argument (not to be confused with the virtue argument) has long been the central argument. It says: it is the moral responsibility of the strong to help the weak, of the rich to help the poor, of the privileged to help the disadvantaged. With respect to early childhood, the moral argument recognizes that quality parenting is the index of advantage, and therefore those who have experienced the privilege of loving, structured nurture have a moral responsibility to help those who lack such loving nurture. Virtually everyone I know who has become personally involved in serving families of disadvantaged young children through coaching, tutoring, mentoring, foster care, adoption, early intervention and education has done so because they *feel* the moral imperative to serve these children and families.

The economic argument has advanced in recent years alongside the moral argument. Art Rolnick, the co-director for the Human Capital Research Collaborative at the University of Minnesota, first became involved in early childhood research and advocacy because the Director of a Minnesota non-profit, *Ready for Kindergarten,* appealed for investment in early childhood policy on the basis of the moral argument. As an economist, Rolnick wanted more; he wanted to know whether investments in early childhood made economic sense. In his research, he found that economic investment in early childhood development had a very, very high return on investment, far surpassing the returns from investment in later education. Rolnick concluded: there are strong moral arguments for a host of educational programs from birth to post-secondary education. However, the economic argument for investment in early childhood is what sets it ahead of appeals for funds for primary, secondary and post-secondary education. Investment in children in the earliest years of their lives serves them – and their communities, and society – better than other investments.

The virtue argument, which I have presented here, is distinct from the moral argument and in fact clarifies and directs the moral argument. The moral argument centers on the responsibility of the advantaged to help the disadvantaged. The virtue argument centers on the dignity of the disadvantaged – both parents and children – and the role of parents in forming the character of their children during the earliest years of life. It is they, the disadvantaged parents, who develop virtue by making hard (and good) choices for the sake of their children. It is they who nurture their children's virtue by establishing their children's experience of normal and normative. An individual or organization can respond the moral argument by seeking to help disadvantaged children; yet if they do not heed the virtue argument, they may unwittingly undermine the dignity of those they purport to help, and discourage rather than encourage the cultivation of virtue. Those who heed *both* the moral argument and the virtue argument will act *with* disadvantaged parents and children in ways that affirm their dignity, treat them as responsible, and cherish their meaningful contributions to family, community and society.

Moreover, those who respond to the moral and virtue arguments will celebrate those families in which they see virtue flourishing. In my final year of teaching I had a delightful second grade student named Heather. She was respectful, helpful and hard-working. She needed to work hard, because classroom learning didn't come as readily to her as it did to some of her classmates, and yet she persevered, which impressed me. I was shocked to learn that Heather was one of ten children – ten children of the same parents. All ten children lived with their parents in a three bedroom apartment in the Brooklyn neighborhood where I lived and taught. I learned from other teachers in my school that Heather's siblings shared her reputation – kind, courteous, and diligent. How did it happen? Why were these children so exemplary when they had so many obvious pressures on them? Heather's parents modeled the kind of virtue that they nurtured in their children. They were not wealthy by any stretch of the imagination (her father drove a shuttle van to and from the NYC airports), and yet they created a family culture of love and learning.

Heather's family is a demonstration of how the moral, economic and virtue arguments can and must intertwine. They demonstrate that families with limited resources can and do raise beautiful, virtuous children who contribute to the life of a community. They show that the investment that parents make in their children have a marked social, civic, and economic impact on the community by preventing potential social costs, *and* by equipping their children to play a constructive role in their family, school, community and society. Indeed, anyone who has met Heather's parents realizes that the moral argument to help disadvantaged children *must* treat parents as responsible and equip them rather than marginalizing their role by attempting to replace them. Heather's parents are a vivid demonstration of courageous, beautiful parenting – as measured by the difficulty of raising ten responsible, kind children in a three bedroom Brooklyn apartment.

# CHAPTER 9

# Apprenticeship: Examples and Exceptions

At an exhibition tennis match featuring Andre Agassi and Andy Roddick, Roddick served a blazing ace. From the audience, someone heckled Agassi, "My grandmother could have gotten that!" Since it was an exhibition match, Agassi stopped and asked the crowd who had yelled out. The man's neighbors singled him out. Andre Agassi had him come down on the court and try to return an Andy Roddick serve. Not surprisingly, the man couldn't even get his racket back by the time the ball whizzed past him, much less hit or return it.

In much the same way, heckling education reformers from the stands is poor form. Rather than shouting down those who work hard day in and day out in schools, daycare centers, after-school programs, drop-in centers, job training initiatives, and juvenile halls, I want to offer positive examples of where the principle of apprenticeship is being embraced in ways that transform families and communities. And I want to address a "rock star" counter-example that might be held up against the apprenticeship thesis.

## A Double Example: Geoffrey Canada & The Baby College

Geoffrey Canada is a rising star in the conversation surrounding education and parental development. New York City Mayor Mike Bloomberg called him the most important living New Yorker.[xxiv] Canada, one of four brothers, was born and raised in the South Bronx by his mother amidst crime, drugs, violence and chaos after his father abandoned the family. Despite these challenges, his mother did not abdicate her parental responsibilities, but tutored her sons, limited their television viewing and intentionally cultivated their character. When Geoffrey was fifteen, his mother sent him to live with her parents on Long Island, where he attended high school. Canada earned a bachelor's degree from Bowdoin College and a Master's Degree in Education from Harvard University before returning to help disadvantaged kids in Harlem. Over the past twenty years, Canada's work has become the *Harlem Children's Zone*, one of the most successful and celebrated organizations to tackle the many dimensions of cyclical poverty.

The cornerstone of the *Harlem Children's Zone* is the *Baby College*, a nine-week parenting workshop for expectant parents and those raising a child up to three years old. Not only is it free, but outreach workers walk the streets and tour public housing sites to invite parents who would not otherwise seek out such opportunities. In the workshops, parents learn about brain development and the importance of language and reading. They discuss the challenges of parenting and provide support to one another. The *Baby College* is the first step on the *Harlem Children's Zone's* "conveyor belt" from birth to college. Parents from the *Baby College* who receive a lottery seat in the Promise Academy charter schools are then welcomed into the *Three Year Old Journey*, which continues the process of helping parents to cultivate parenting skills in order to help their children build language abilities. Throughout this period, HCZ is investing money not in daycare centers, but intentionally and directly in parents.

By this time the stage is set for the children to participate in the six-week *Get Ready for Pre-K* class before they begin the *Harlem Gems*, the HCZ's full day pre-kindergarten program which includes instruction in Spanish, French and English, and a 4:1 child-to-teacher ratio. By the time a child enters kindergarten at one of the Promise Academies, HCZ has already invested deeply in parents – knowing well that their involvement is the best predictor of their children's educational achievement.

Geoffrey Canada's childhood experience is an example of the power of apprenticeship, and his work in the Harlem Children's Zone is an outstanding model of recognizing and harnessing the power of apprenticeship in the earliest years by engaging and empowering parents. Canada speaks freely about the tremendous influence that his mother had on him, as well as his initiation and indoctrination into the street fighting culture of his South Bronx ghetto in his gripping memoir *Fist, Stick, Knife, Gun: A Personal History of Violence in America.* He is a brilliant example of the influence and interplay of *both* family culture and street culture. From those experiences, Canada is now establishing the dignity and responsibility of parents in his community by empowering them for their responsibility in a direct attempt to prevent their children from being initiated into destructive cultures like the violent, father-absent, drug-pushing one he experienced in the South Bronx. The result? By grade 3, 93% of the students in the Promise Academies meet or exceed the grade level standards in English Language Arts, and 100% meet or exceed the grade standards in math.[xxv] The *Harlem Children Zone* tackled the parenting gap head on. And it *eliminated* the achievement gap.

## An International Example: Parents as Teachers

*Parents as Teachers* (PAT) is an international organization that helps local organizations and professionals support parents during the critical early years of their children's lives, from conception to kindergarten. *PAT* works in all fifty states and seven other countries through its in-home *Born to Learn* visitation program. Unlike the *Harlem Children's Zone*, it doesn't just serve one community or just disadvantaged families (although they strategically plan to reach the most vulnerable families). What makes *PAT* unique and remarkable is its conviction that *all* parents can benefit from the support of professional in-home visits to understand child development, recognize developmental delays and health issues (in order to receive early intervention), and support a life-long love of learning. By serving all parents, there is no sense that "You're a bad parent, so you need professional help." Instead, they embody their core value: "Parents are their children's first and most influential teachers."

As a result, participation in *Parents as Teachers* predicts children's school readiness and third grade achievement, regardless of income level. Parents in the *Parents as Teachers* program read more frequently to their young children

70

and were more likely to enroll their children in preschool, both of which were positively linked to school readiness and later school achievement. Consequently,

> A large percentage (82%) of poor children who participated with high intensity in both Parents as Teachers and preschool entered kindergarten ready to learn, as compared to only 64% of poor children who had no involvement in either service. A similar pattern emerged for more affluent children (93% vs. 81%).[xxvi]

Like the *Harlem Children's Zone, Parents as Teachers* recognizes the dignity and responsibility of parents, and informs and equips them to fulfill their crucial role. In the world of early nurture, *Parents as Teachers* is demonstrating that "an ounce of prevention is worth a pound of cure."

## Exception That Proves the Rule: Roland G. Fryer

At the age of 30, economist Roland G. Fryer Jr. became the youngest African American professor to receive tenure at Harvard University. In December 2008, *The Economist* named Fryer as one of the top 8 young economists in the world. From where did this gifted scholar arise? Born in Daytona Beach, Florida, Fryer's mother and father separated when he was only three years old. In his father's custody, and without his mother's knowledge, he grew up in Lewisville, Texas. Fryer returned to Daytona Beach to spend summers with his grandmother. There he frequently visited his great-aunt, who ran a profitable crack house. "One day, [when he was 12] Fryer dawdled on his way there, and arrived to see the house surrounded by law-enforcement officials; nearly everyone in the household went to prison for their involvement in the illegal dealings."[xxvii] One family member died in prison, and another was murdered not long after being released. By age 13, Fryer himself was selling marijuana and carrying a gun. He excelled in sports, and emerged as a standout athlete in high school, despite the fact that his father drank heavily, was abusive, and during those years was convicted of sexual assault.

Fryer's athletic prowess brought him to the University of Texas at Arlington on an athletic scholarship, and there he discovered his aptitude for learning. He graduated *magna cum laude* with a degree in economics in two and a half years – while holding down a full-time job.[xxviii] By age 25, he had completed his PhD at Penn State, and received a three-year research fellowship at Harvard University, after which he became an associate, and then tenured, professor. Fryer is now using his considerable intellectual and social capital to pursue, as the *New York Times Magazine* called it, "A Unified Theory of Black America."

So, is Roland Fryer a glaring counter-example who unravels the thesis that early childhood is the apprenticeship of being human? On the contrary, he is the exception that proves the rule. If Fryer's achievements were normal for a person of his upbringing, they would not be worthy of notice. It is precisely the magnitude of his disadvantage (measured by quality of parenting) that makes his achievements so admirable. Statistically, Fryer should be an under-educated, gun-toting, drug-vending felon. The fact that he is one of the top young economists in the world should both guard against the foolish fatalism that suggests children who have disadvantaged childhoods can't accomplish anything *and* reinforce Frederick Douglass' famous maxim, "It is easier to build strong children than to repair broken men." Just ask any of Roland's high school classmates who have spent significant parts of their lives behind bars.

# CHAPTER 10

## Truly Social Justice

*"Only when every individual in a community shoulders the burden of maintaining justice can it be 'social' in any true sense."*

Noel Bouché, *Exploited: Sex Trafficking, Porn Culture, and the Call to a Lifestyle of Justice*

If it is true that early childhood is the apprenticeship of being human, and that the dignity of parents is bound up in their responsibility to love, protect and teach their children, then *social justice* must mean that *every* member of the family, community and society shoulders the burden of cultivating virtue and establishing justice. To diminish the importance, role, or responsibility of any member is to deprecate their dignity – thereby further undermining a truly just social order. Far from playing a blame game, understanding social justice as the reciprocal responsibilities of citizens is essential to enabling each to fulfill his or her responsibilities.

In the introduction I said that parents are the core of my intended audience because they are the primary stakeholders in education, and the *chief culture architects* of their families. In addition to the unparalleled influence they have in their families, parents also have notable influence in their first-ring circle of friends and neighbors – many of whom are also parents. The people who most influence me in my parenting choices are those I know best and trust most fully. They do it by modeling, encouragement, reproof, handing me a good book, or by recommending a community resource.

Now, in conclusion, I will address some of the many important stakeholders in social justice by asking: What can each group do to fulfill its own role and strengthen the others? I will deliberately move from society to community to family, recognizing that larger-scale change will have the greatest impact by empowering the health of the smallest groups.

## Society Level: Policy Makers & Advocates

### Business Leaders

Educators aren't the only ones who care about education. Numerous business leaders and organizations lobby for investment in early education, nurture and intervention. *Ready Nation* (formerly *The Partnership for America's Economic Success*) is one such coalition of economists, policy experts, and advocates mobilizing business leaders to make policy investments in young children. They understand well that current investments in early childhood pay manifold returns in the quality of the workforce fifteen to twenty years from now. The question is how these leaders can use their cultural capital to the greatest positive influence.

Business leaders can best build human capital by investments in initiatives and programs like *Parents as Teachers* that engage and empower parents, foster early diagnosis of disabilities, and connect parents with available resources, such as library story times, parenting networks, early intervention, and preschool programs. By investing in early childhood *through* families, they strengthen the single best predictor of children's educational achievement: parent involvement. That is why billionaire Stanley Drunkenmiller is chair of the *Harlem Children's Zone* board and invests so deeply to the organization. He's demonstrating that early investment in parents delivers the best return on investment.

### Military Leaders

What would inspire the retired NATO supreme commander and retired top brass of the US military to form *Mission: Readiness*, an organization devoted to promoting early childhood education? At present, seventy-five percent of young people ages 17 to 24 are unable to enlist in the military because they fail to graduate high school, have a criminal record, or are physically unfit.[xxix] These military leaders recognize that the trajectory of young people is set very, very early and are lobbying hard for high quality early education programs – particularly for the most at-risk children in order that there might be at least a few ready, willing and able to serve in the armed forces.

In addition to supporting initiatives that strengthen the family in early childhood, it is just as critical for military leaders to champion the importance of character. The *Medal of Honor* is the United States' highest medal for valor in combat that can be awarded to members of the armed forces. It is not merely competence that is recognized and decorated, but outstanding courage and honor. Children learn from the cradle whether integrity and honor are worthy values by what their parents and community celebrate and honor. It is truly and deeply in the national interest that honor, courage and integrity be nurtured in every home.

## Community Level: Educators

### Researchers

In addition to the many teachers and administrators who devote themselves to the love of learning, there are many others who serve the cause through research. One such organization is the *Harvard Family Research Project* (HFRP), which strengthens family, school and community partnerships by researching and disseminating best practices to policymakers, teachers, administrators and philanthropists. Their concern is not merely with the theory of child development, but the practice. What *really* works in advantaged and disadvantaged communities to foster the strongest relationships among families, schools, early intervention, daycare, after-school programs and remediation?

It hardly needs to be said that researchers work toward the "sweet spot" where time, energy and money are optimally spent in promoting lifetime character, competence, creativity, health and collaboration. At this point, one of the most important questions that researchers can and should be asking is, "What works *and doesn't cost a fortune?*" Roland Fryer has praised the *Harlem*

*Children's Zone's* elimination of the achievement gap as "the equivalent of the curing cancer for these kids."[xxx] Critics, however, have pointed out that the HCZ, with two billionaires on its board of directors, has more resources than any similar organization can hope or expect to have. So the pressing question is: "How can we do it on a reasonable, sustainable budget?"

## Reformers

Most of the education reform movement is, understandably, focused on K-12 education. Teachers, administrators, and educational entrepreneurs naturally focus in on their own populations: students in kindergarten through twelfth grade. And since the vast majority of schools have separate administration for elementary, middle and high school, the sets of needs and issues is further compartmentalized. Early intervention for a two-year-old today doesn't directly affect the high school principal in whose school sixteen-year-old students are *currently* reading at a fourth grade level, and yet still need to pass their exams. And in fourteen years, when that two-year-old is a sophomore in high school, chances are that the current principal won't be around any longer. Since the social costs of failing to intervene early are so widely distributed among schools, after-school programs, job training initiatives, prisons, public housing, health care, food stamps and other programs, it is understandable that achieving united investment in families in the earliest years is extraordinarily difficult.

For education reform to achieve its aim, it must seize the two most important levers – early nurture and parent involvement – while not losing sight of its mission and mandate to provide a robust, rigorous education to its current students. The *Harlem Children's Zone* provides an example of a "conveyor belt" model that achieves this aim by integrating all of the pieces from birth to high school in one network. It works precisely because it starts at birth – and begins with parents.

In Minnesota, *Early Childhood Family Education* is an example of a successful initiative that works through the public schools to offer classes for parents and children from birth through kindergarten. Although not a conveyor belt, it strategically uses existing resources in communities to equip and empower parents from birth. Whether the mechanism is charter schools, public schools, non-profit organizations or something else, reformers must find creative ways to use existing resources to support and involve parents from birth while bridging the leadership gaps among elementary, middle and high school education – to say nothing of the myriad social service organizations that support children and families.

## Family Level: Parents

Any parent who has more than one child can tell you that two children of the same parents can be shockingly different – in temperament, interests, and abilities (and disabilities). There isn't a magic formula that works for all children. Indeed, one of the most careless ways to understand the apprenticeship thesis is to treat it as a formula. That plays into a foolish determinism that says, "If a child doesn't have a supportive environment, he is doomed to delinquency and imprisonment," *and,* just as foolishly, "If a child has a loving, language-rich environment, she will flourish in all areas of civic responsibility." As a formula, the apprenticeship thesis fails miserably; as a metaphor for understanding and harnessing the nature of early childhood, it suggests ways for parents to wisely engage their children *differently.*

### Reflection, Resolve & Repetition

The beginning of a new year often creates an interesting impetus for change. Many people take time to reflect on the past year, form resolutions for the year to come, and plan routines by which to accomplish those resolutions. For parents, this process of reflection, resolve and repetition doesn't need to happen just once a year. It can become part of the fabric of family life on a regular basis. *Where are we in a rut? What has become normal in our home that needs to change? What daily or weekly routines can we establish that solidify the kind of norms and normal experience we want for our children?* Perhaps it is a weekly family game night to encourage playing together. (Have you ever noticed how social games like *Balderdash, Scattegories, Catch Phrase* and *Cranium* draw upon and expand verbal abilities in the context of lively, social games?) Another family might choose to read aloud together after dinner. Yet another might sign up to do a service project together with *Habitat for Humanity.* Is there any family that would not benefit from a regular discipline of reflection, resolve and repetition?

Like New Year's Resolutions, parental leadership that is not characterized by reflection, resolve and repetition is little more than wishful thinking.

## Love, Language and Literature

When reflecting on what ruts to break, and what routines to establish, it is helpful to consider how routines foster love, language, and love for literature. One of the simplest ways to begin is with a family meal. I had the privilege, a few years ago, of interviewing remarkable people for a podcast series for parents of young children. In that podcast series, three very different people pointed me to the family meal. Gladys Hunt, the author of *Honey for a Child's Heart: The Imaginative Use of Books in Family Life* made the bold contention that,

> The most serious problem with television is not its programs (although that is a subject worth discussion), but its destruction of the average family's exchange of views and information at the evening meal.

Likewise, Ellyn Satter, the author of *Child of Mine: Feeding with Love and Good Sense* suggested to me that the first and most important step a family can take toward eating well is to establish the routine of a family meal. Why? Eating together is an important context in which we learn to talk to one another, affirm each other, and yes, even read together. In fact, Ellen will go so far as to say that *how* parents structure the family meal (sitting together at the table, without electronic interruptions, etc.) is even more important than *what* goes on the table when you begin the routine.

The third guest on my podcast was Noah Blumenthal, who was named one of the "Top 100 Minds in Personal Development" by *Leadership Magazine.* I asked Noah how he maintained a vibrant family life in the midst of building a consulting business, writing books, and speaking at conferences. His answer? Their family meal is sacred. Each night at dinner they turn off all the interruption devices – TV, radio, phones, computer, etc. – and talk to each other over dinner. When I hear three leading thinkers from diverse fields impress upon me the importance of a single practice (despite very different lines of questioning), it gives me pause for reflection.

The beauty of cultivating love, language and the enjoyment of literature in the family is that it is the opposite of teaching to the test; it simply *is* life.

Far from pulling out flashcards at the dinner table, it is sharing a fun poem (What child can resist the playful language and illustrations of Shel Silverstein?), or asking a pressing question (Why do we have homework?!), or recounting a memorable experience (Today the coolest thing happened . . .). These authentic, repeated experiences enlarge children's vocabularies, broaden their horizons, and encourage them to consider and embrace what is truly valuable.

## Character, Competence, Creativity & Collaboration

When I taught in the New York City public schools, I had some students from tough backgrounds. Some were emotionally disturbed. Some (including the emotionally disturbed) already outweighed me; and they were only in the third grade. However, there was one group of students that broke the mold: those who were "fresh off the boat" from the Caribbean. No matter how far behind they were, my students who arrived from the Islands understood how to respect teachers and fellow students. They were polite and hardworking, and a delight to teach because they were raised in a culture where respect for teachers is one of the highest values. I would, in a heartbeat, take a class of 30 well-disciplined, respectful students over a group of 15 who were disrespectful. I'd even take the larger class *and* a smaller budget over the smaller class of unruly students. Why? Where there are respectful, reciprocal, responsible relationships, children (and their communities) learn and flourish. Character is the fertile soil in which competence, creativity and the ability to collaborate grow.

When parents reflect on how to establish a culture of respect and virtue in the home, they lay the foundation for thriving relationships and a lifelong love of learning in all spheres of life, including the classroom.

# Love Your Neighbor

There are many people who don't fall into any of the above categories. They are not societal leaders or community leaders. Nor do they have young children. What does the apprenticeship of being human have to do with them?

They are neighbors; *we* are neighbors. In Jesus' famous Parable of the Good Samaritan, a man traveling from Jerusalem to Jericho was attacked by robbers who left him half dead. Three men happened upon him. The first, a priest, "when he saw him, passed by on the other side" of the road. The second, a Levite, did likewise. The third was a Samaritan, and "when he saw him, he had compassion. He went to him and bound up his wounds, pouring on oil and wine. Then he set him on his own animal and brought him to an inn and took care of him. And the next day he took out two denarii [roughly two days wages] and gave them to the innkeeper, saying, 'Take care of him, and whatever more you spend, I will repay you when I come back.'"

Jesus asked, "Which of these three, do you think, proved to be a neighbor to the man who fell among the robbers?" The man to whom he had told the story replied, "The one who showed him mercy." And Jesus said to him, "You go, and do likewise."

This story upsets our expectations at many levels. We expect the first two men, who shared the same nationality as the injured man, and held respected positions in society, to show mercy; yet they do not. We think that our neighbors are just those near us; yet in this story it is the despised foreigner who "proved to be a neighbor." We think of neighbors as *other* people to whom we relate; here we are told that we are to *be* neighbors.

Jesus told this story in answer to a direct question, "And who is my neighbor?" The command to love your neighbor as yourself is at the heart of truly social justice. If, as James Heckman contends, parenting quality is the best measure of advantage and disadvantage in contemporary society, then loving parents of young children by supporting and equipping them in that role may be one of the most powerful ways to *be* a neighbor. Indeed, I wouldn't be surprised if, like the priest and Levite, many societal and community leaders "pass by on the other side" of the parents in need, and others – singles, divorcees, empty nesters, foster parents, retirees, teachers, mentors, coaches, and others – are the ones who prove to *be* neighbors by coming alongside parents of young children. Like bandaging a stranger who has been robbed and left for dead, it can be messy and costly. Such is real love for one's neighbors, without which there can be no truly social justice.

Leaving a rewarding job in the financial services to teach in a challenging school was, for me, one step in learning to love my neighbors. It was painful and fraught with failure, as I blundered through my first years of teaching. My students, their parents, and my fellow teachers can tell stories, both funny and sad, of my foibles. And yet in those stories, I hope, there is the consistent strain of love. I was willing to persevere in learning to be a good teacher, in supporting parents, in learning from my colleagues for the good of my neighbors. In doing so, I hope to offer an example of what I desire for the families that we served: progress in process. Just as I didn't become a good teacher overnight, I couldn't expect the parents of my students to flip a switch and suddenly become outstanding parents. For both of us, the path of cultivating virtue is one that requires discipline, patience, and a supportive community.

As a member of that virtue-seeking community, I have written three appendixes for our common benefit. The first, *Underlying Classism?,* explains why seeing educational failure as "their problem" is both wrong and classist, and offers a positive vision in which the responsibility and dignity of both the privileged and disadvantaged are preserved. The second, *The Practice of Parenting* is a very practical tool for parents and those who support them to recognize how the principles of apprenticeship operate in *their* families, and to deliberately establish routines that nurture healthy relationships. It is designed to be used, and re-used in the routine of reflection, resolve and repetition. The final appendix *Recommended Resources* points readers to a short list of books, articles and web resources for further reading. Finally, the *Afterword* is a call to arms that draws on the courage and innovation of leaders in other spheres to be applied to the cultivation of virtue in the family in the most dynamic and influential years of life.

I am inviting you, in the name of love, to engage personally in a movement of social renewal that we desperately need. I'm not just inviting you to vote for a candidate who will fund early childhood programs (although I hope that you will see how important it is as a public policy issue and make it an issue with political candidates and elected officials). Nor am I asking you merely to donate to worthy organizations like *The Ounce of Prevention Fund* or *Zero to Three* (although I hope that you will give generously to organizations like these). Donations are good, but they can also be a way of avoiding more personal engagement with the issues. Nor am I asking you simply to "click here" to sign an online petition for parent support. Rather, I am inviting you to embrace the responsibility and joys of parenting – and of being a neighbor to parents of young children. Read *The Practice of Parenting* appendix; share it and use it. It is much harder than going to the polling station, or writing a check, or clicking on a web petition – and it has a far greater impact on the wellbeing of children, the health of communities, and the flourishing of society. The difficulty of the task is the index of the measure of virtue you show in loving your neighbors.

# Appendix 1

## Underlying Classism?

There is a growing tribe of writers like Bryan Caplan, an economist at George Mason University, who argue that parenting only matters for the poor.[xxxi] Statistically, they say, intervention with poor parents is very effective; but the differences in outcomes among middle and upper-middle class children are marginal. Wealthier kids turn out fine regardless of whether their parents were helicopter parents or free range parents.[10] The line roughly goes, "Of course neglected kids in orphanages and poor children of drug addicts benefit from improved parenting because their environments are appalling! But middle- and upper-middle class parents aren't popping needles or planning on sending their kids to orphanages." On this line of thinking, books on parenting really don't matter for the very parents who read them. *Freakonomics* co-authors Steven D. Levitt and Stephen J. Dubner summarize,

---

[10] "Helicopter parents" is a colloquialism for parents who "hover" over their children in an attempt to protect them. By contrast, "free range parents" intentionally give their children freedom and responsibility and withdraw from oversight.

"[I]t isn't so much a matter of what you *do* as a parent; it's who you are." In this argument, there is both truth and distortion.

As I said at the beginning, apprenticeship is not a parenting program or technique to be employed in order to have happy, successful, well-adjusted children. Rather, it is a metaphor that describes the dynamics of human development in early childhood (and beyond) regardless of what parenting methods are employed. As a metaphor, it is a hearty endorsement of Levitt and Dubner's conclusion: parenting isn't about tricks or techniques; it is fundamentally about who you are, and the fact that your little apprentices are learning from you and imitating you as they learn how to make their way in the world.

However, there are at least two threads of distortion in saying parenting only matters for kids in poverty. First, it tends to put competence ahead of character in the ordering of values. If a student cheats (does not use a good means) in order to excel in school, he has not enriched his family, community and society. If another student shows integrity in her studies and then uses her learning to devise collateralized debt obligations that deliberately hide risk from investors (not a good end), she has harmed and not helped her community and society, regardless of her annual income. Educational achievement and economic stability are important, but are not sufficient proxies for virtue and social contribution.

The second distortion of the argument that parenting only matters for the poor is that it denigrates the importance of practice. No one becomes excellent in a chosen field without resolved, reflective repetition. In fact, no one becomes *anything* without practice. What we do repeatedly – well or poorly – shapes who we are. When I lived in Brooklyn, I played basketball on the outdoor courts at the local high school with some amazing athletes. How did these guys (many of whom clearly didn't have jobs in the formal economy) become so good? They spent hours upon hours on the court. They watched college and professional games on TV and imitated their heroes. Or consider the kids who hang out on the street corner instead of going to school, who can recite entire albums by *50 Cent* – with passion! Clearly, many kids in poverty are not incapable of remarkable learning and excellence.[11] Rather the forces of *desire, delight,* and *discipline* have as their object something other than classroom learning and community development. Who your parents are – manifested by what they do (or don't do) – has an enormous influence on what you practice, and how you practice.

The principle of disciplined practice is at work at every level of income, in every zip code, and in every pursuit. Again, as in the first distortion (measuring success merely by academic achievement), the question is where that passion is applied. Is it applied to basketball, or selling drugs, or to restoring communities? Of course, what you choose depends on your Story. What *really* matters? Is it basketball, or fingernails? Or driving a BMW? Or living in the right zip code? Or getting into the right college? Or going to the best vacation spots? The Stories of wealthier families influence their children's pursuits and practice no less than the Stories that animate the parents of their poorer peers. To say that parenting matters only for the poor is not only untrue; it is a subtle form of classism.

While early childhood functions as the apprenticeship of being human in *all* families, regardless of zip code, ethnicity or class, it is arguable that the influence that parents in wealthier families wield actually matters more, not less. Why? Children of wealthier parents will, by default, have more cultural influence at the community and societal levels – influence which can be abused, squandered, or employed for the common good. These children will be the ones who can invest their time in mentoring and tutoring. They are the ones who will have the rhetorical ability to convince others to act *with* struggling families to break cycles of poverty. Or, tragically, they may be the ones to pursue their own prosperity without any care for others.

That, in the end, is the trouble with the argument that parenting differences matter only among the poor. It ignores the fact that our animating Stories influence where we live, how we live, and how we raise our children. The fact that wealthier families have a wider range of choices within which to exercise this freedom means that their children will have a greater

---

[11] Learning disabilities *do* afflict many children, and have a compounded effect on children who lack a supportive home environment, which only makes their situation more desperate. My intent here is simply to recognize the many ways in which children *do* apply themselves passionately to certain sorts of self-directed learning.

range of possibilities to cultivate, squander or exploit their cultural inheritance and influence. For every wealthy kid who is a peer tutor for a struggling student, how many others are viewing internet porn, sexting, or listening to pirated music? To suggest that parenting only matters for the poor is naïve, classist, and destructive.

That is precisely why I have written a book about the importance of early childhood parenting primarily for educated persons, and particularly educated parents. Their decisions matter more, not less, because:

1. It is within the power of educated parents to influence the virtue and values of their own children.
2. Educated persons have influence among their family, friends, neighbors and community to nurture character, competence, creativity and collaboration.
3. Educated persons have the abilities and cultural power to find ways to empower and help parents in poverty through friendship, vocation, volunteering, philanthropy, advocacy and policy.

In my years of teaching in Brooklyn, it struck me more than once that it was very likely for a second grade student of mine to have never witnessed a healthy marriage. In fact, it was very possible that many of my students didn't know anyone whose parents were married when they were born and were still married. In short, it was *normal* for my students to have half-siblings whose fathers they had not met, and to have no meaningful relationship with their own fathers.[12] If the parents who most need encouragement and good role models (like the parents of my students) are those who – by definition – have the least access to mentors, coaches, and role models within their own community, who can better fill this role than compassionate individuals who have had the privilege of good role models and a supportive community? This is truly how the "advantaged" can serve the "disadvantaged" in a way that recognizes how staggering a disadvantage it is to lack modeling and

---

[12]Thankfully, there were exceptions to the norm of father-absence in my school. Two fathers in particular come to mind who were both present and involved. Their children thrived – even with a young teacher in a "school in need of improvement."

support, *and* affirms the dignity and courage of parents who have never had those advantages.

For this reason, I have included the following appendix called *The Practice of Parenting*. It is an exercise for *all* parents in considering how they establish their children's expectations of normal and normative — and what changes they might make to establish healthy routines. It is not classist in saying, "This is a tool for fixing screwed-up families." On the contrary, my assumption is truly that early childhood parenting matters for *everyone*.

# Appendix 2

# The Practice of Parenting

The apprenticeship of being human is a metaphor, not a method. It is, however, a metaphor with meaning. Parents can and should use this metaphor to examine their parenting methods. In this appendix, I offer a simple sequence of questions for parents to consider how they influence their children . . .

**In:** *Character, competence, creativity and the ability to collaborate*

**Through:** *Love, language and literature*

**By:** *Reflection, resolve and repetition.*

---

Charles and his mother visited the pediatrician for his annual checkup. At eight years of age, Charles tipped the scales at over 180 pounds. In previous visits to the doctor, Charles and his mother had discussed his obesity. In this visit, the doctor asked Charles' mother if she had followed through on the dietary recommendations they had discussed at the previous visit. In exasperation, his mother said, "He buys himself Philly cheese steaks!"

Charles and his mother are both decision makers, and their decisions have consequences for Charles' lifelong health. In fact, their decisions have consequences for a whole constellation of other people, including taxpayers and medical insurance subscribers. One scholarly estimate puts the annual medical burden of obesity at ten percent of all medical spending and almost $147 billion dollars per year.[xxxii] At times, it is tempting for parents to abdicate and say, "It is my child's fault!" However, as in the case of Charles, parents function as the gatekeepers. An eight year old can only buy Philly cheesesteaks if he has money; and regardless of pleadings to the contrary, parents hold the purse strings. The way we make decisions as parents teaches our children how to make decisions. Our children are apprenticed to us in the development of *agency*, the capacity of an individual to make meaningful choices in the world.

If indeed early childhood is the apprenticeship of being human and early childhood parenting matters to everyone in society, what can be done? Just as children's repeated experiences establish what is normal and normative, so also the repeated practices of parenting establish *our* sense of normal and express (in some degree) what we believe to be normative. What follows is an exercise in recognizing our repeated experiences, identifying patterns over which we have influence, and beginning the process of establishing routines that embody what we *want* to be normal and normative in our families.

# Step 1: Reflection

## Ruts and Grooves

When we find ourselves in a pattern we don't like, we often say, "I'm stuck in a rut." When we're in a rhythm that we want to continue, we say, "I'm getting in the groove!" Whether the trench is a rut or a groove depends on whether it is a good pattern or a bad one. For parents, it is helpful to frequently ask:

1.  Where are we in a rut?
2.  Where are we in a groove?

Start by thinking about the things that you do every day as related to the three key factors in child development:

### *Love, Language and Literature*

"I love you," is one of the most important sentences a child can hear. A child's repeated experience of loving language in the home shapes her posture toward language. Is language merely a means for getting what I want? Or is it for putting others in their place? Or is it for exploring and enjoying the world? The way we repeatedly use language at home invariably shapes the way our children will use language.

Ask yourself:

1. How do I *usually* express love for my children?

- Hugs and kisses?
- Saying "I love you"?
- Listening to them?
- Doing things for them (like packing lunches)?
- Making things (like a favorite meal)?

| Love | |
|---|---|
| **Grooves** | |
| **Ruts** | |

2. What are the ways that we *regularly* converse as a family?
   - What do we talk about at meal times?
   - What do we enjoy talking about?
   - When do we have the best conversations?
   - How do we resolve conflict?
   - How do we enjoy having fun with words?

| Language | |
|---|---|
| **Grooves** | |
| | |
| | |
| | |
| | |
| | |
| **Ruts** | |
| | |
| | |
| | |
| | |
| | |

3. What role do stories play in our family life?
   - When do we enjoy books together?
   - When do we tell – and listen to – stories?
   - When do we enjoy words in poems or songs?
   - What stories told on screen (movies, TV) shape our life?
   - What stories have shaped our shared vocabulary?

| Literature | |
|---|---|
| **Grooves** | |
| | |
| | |
| | |
| | |
| | |
| **Ruts** | |
| | |
| | |
| | |
| | |
| | |

Love, language and literature are the three key areas that you influence. But they're not the only realms of family life in which you may be in a rut or a groove. It may be that mealtime is mayhem, and you recognize you're in a rut. Or you may realize that reading books with your child at bedtime is your favorite part of every day. You've found a groove. Before long you'll probably have a list of at least 5 or 6 areas you're in a rut or a groove.

| Ruts | Grooves |
|------|---------|
| 1 | 1 |
| 2 | 2 |
| 3 | 3 |
| 4 | 4 |
| 5 | 5 |
| 6 | 6 |

## Normal & Normative

Now you're in the position to ask how these patterns influence your children:

1. How do these routines establish a sense of *normal*?
2. How do our routines teach what is *normative*?

For example, "In our house, it is normal to read books together before bedtime. This teaches our kids that we love spending time with them and that beautiful stories are valuable and enjoyable." It can be helpful to name it by writing it out, even in a few words:

| | Rut/Groove | Normal/ Normative |
|---|---|---|
| 1 | | |
| 2 | | |
| 3 | | |
| 4 | | |
| 5 | | |
| 6 | | |
| 7 | | |

# Step 2: Resolve

## Character, Competence, Creativity & Collaboration

Knowing your ruts and grooves is half the battle. You can already see where your repeated actions have influence in both positive and negative ways. Now it is time to move from where you are to where you want to be in the four key areas that you influence: character, competence, creativity and the ability to collaborate.

What are the specific virtues, abilities, and qualities that you want to nurture in your children? You'll find some fit squarely in one category, and others could easily fall into multiple buckets. Using the four categories can help you think of qualities and abilities that might not otherwise have occurred to you.

Here are some suggestions to spark reflection: *love, humility, courage, patience, kindness, gentleness, compassion, generosity, loyalty, honor, justice, wisdom, self-control, contentment, gratitude, honesty, integrity, joyfulness, modesty, perseverance, simplicity, trustworthiness, resourcefulness, responsibility, active listening, diligence, inquisitiveness, respect, and peacemaking.*

| Character | | Competence | |
|---|---|---|---|
| 1 | | 1 | |
| 2 | | 2 | |
| 3 | | 3 | |
| 4 | | 4 | |
| 5 | | 5 | |
| 6 | | 6 | |
| 7 | | 7 | |

| Creativity | | Collaboration | |
|---|---|---|---|
| 1 | | 1 | |
| 2 | | 2 | |
| 3 | | 3 | |
| 4 | | 4 | |
| 5 | | 5 | |
| 6 | | 6 | |
| 7 | | 7 | |

## Indwelling, Initiation and Indoctrination

The qualities and abilities you have listed don't arise out of thin air. They are the outworking of the Story that you indwell, and into which you are initiating and indoctrinating your child. (Remember, indoctrination doesn't mean brainwashing! It means "to instruct especially in the fundamentals or rudiments." We are all indoctrinating our children, whether or not we admit it.) So it can be helpful to pause and ask yourself:

1. What *is* the Story that I indwell?

- How do I decide what is good and valuable?
- How do I decide what is wrong and unworthy?[13]

| Indwelling |
|---|
| |
| |
| |
| |
| |
| |
| |
| |
| |

---

[13] In asking yourself these questions, you may find that you don't like your Story. For example, yours may be the "Power Story" which has animated you to seek power and position above healthy relationships. When you reflect on it, that's not the Story you *want*. That recognition is important. The next – and harder – step is to ask yourself, "What is a worthy Story that truly enables me to become virtuous and cultivate virtue in my children?" That is *The Virtue Problem*, which I will tackle in another book.

2. How am I initiating my children into this Story?
   - How do the stories that we read, tell, and watch shape their vocabulary and understanding of the world?
   - In what ways am I initiating them deliberately, and in what ways am I doing it inadvertently?

| Initiation |
|---|
|  |
|  |
|  |
|  |
|  |
|  |

3. How am I indoctrinating my children into a Story?
   - How am I teaching them the basics of being human?
   - How can I better teach the fundamentals?
   - What stories communicate the Story that I want my children to embrace?

| Indoctrination |
|---|
|  |
|  |
|  |
|  |
|  |

# Step 3: Repetition

As a teacher, I learned "Failing to plan is planning to fail." It is just as true of parents as it is of teachers. The practices of reflection and resolve are incomplete without a plan to implement that resolve in the routines of life. In order to successfully establish those routines, it is important to start small, to focus on the one rut that you want to break, or the one groove that you want to establish.

So what is it? What is the most destructive rut, or the most desirable groove? Or, what is the rut or groove that you think you can most easily change to gain momentum?

| Rut or Groove |
| --- |
|  |
|  |
|  |
|  |
|  |

Next, what *pattern* of life can you change to establish a new routine? My brother and sister-in-law, who are parents of a two-year-old, decided that the groove they wanted to establish in their family was their ideal evening routine. They took inventory of the normal parts of the evening routine: cooking dinner, eating dinner, washing dishes, bath time for the toddler, reading with their daughter, and discretionary time to read, relax or exercise.

In order to establish the routine, they did something surprising. They chose Mondays to implement their new routine. They didn't say, "This is what we're going to do every night from now on!" and then become discouraged when it was just too difficult. By choosing *one* routine to practice on *one* night a week, they created an incubator, a context in which they could practice and refine their routine. They could devote their energies to making Monday evenings work the way they wanted, and then truly enjoy their successes. Once they had successes, they could easily take bits and pieces, like a fun bath routine, and implement them on other nights.

**Desire, Discipline & Delight**

There are three key components to establishing healthy rhythms of life.

1. **Desire.** You've got to want it. If you don't really want to establish a new routine, you won't have the will to follow through. So start with something that you really want.

2. **Discipline.** Changing routines is like turning a gyroscope while it is spinning. It takes work. You can expect resistance; and you can't be entirely sure which way the resistance will push against you.

3. **Delight.** Not only do you need to want it (in desire), you also need to enjoy it. Perhaps you've been persuaded that reading with your children is important, and you *want* to establish a reading routine. Furthermore, you're willing to *work* through the resistance to make it a part of family life. If you don't *like* doing it, your kids probably aren't going to go for it either. Making routines fun for yourself and your kids is important to making them stick.

**Repetition: Do it Again**

Repetition only works if you repeat it. Going through this exercise once can be helpful to parents, but its value will be limited. I once heard a parenting coach ask a group of professionals how often they had a performance review at work. The answers ranged from monthly to annually. The coach then asked, "How often do you sit down to review your performance as parents?" There was an embarrassed silence. We know that performance reviews are important for our vocations because the repeated process forces us to focus on what's going well and what is not. In short, performance reviews help us to identify our ruts and grooves so that we can get out of the ruts and establish good grooves before the next review. However, we rarely apply the same wisdom to parenting. We read a book, or go to a seminar, or meet with a counselor. But we only do it once.

The point is not that you need to use *this* tool for a quarterly review; rather you need some repeated process of reflection, resolve and repetition –

whatever it is. So pick a routine that you really want to establish, that you're committed to doing, and that you will really enjoy. For example, you could start having a family game night. Choose games that you and your children love. Protect the time so that it can't be undermined by work or TV or whatever else usually gets in the way. Then, put a date on the calendar in a month or so to reflect on how the new routine is working. Getting into the routine of reflective parenting will enable you to learn from your failures, celebrate your successes, and establish what you want to be normal and normative in your home.

A printable version of *The Practice of Parenting* can be found at:
www.apprenticeshipofbeinghuman.com/resources/printables/

# APPENDIX 3:
# Recommended Reading

1. **On the Achievement Gap:**
   *Whatever it Takes: Geoffrey Canada's Quest to Change Harlem and America*
   by Paul Tough (especially Chapter 2: Unequal Childhoods)
   *How Children Succeed: Grit, Curiosity, and the Hidden Power of Character*
   by Paul Tough

2. **On Brain Development:**
   Zero to Three
   Harvard Center on the Developing Child

3. **On Stories:**
   *The Call of Stories: Teaching and the Moral Imagination* by Robert Coles
   *Honey for a Child's Heart: The Imaginative Use of Books in Family Life*
   by Gladys Hunt

4. **On Virtue:**
   *After Virtue* by Alisdair MacIntyre (for the philosophically minded)
   *Parenting is Heart Work* by Scott Turansky (for practical counsel)

5. **Early Intervention:**
   www.EarlyInterventionSupport.com
   The Ounce of Prevention Fund (www.ounceofprevention.org)
   Early Childhood Family Education (www.ecfe.info)

6. **Economics:**
   The Heckman Equation (www.HeckmanEquation.org)
   Harvard Center on the Developing Child
   Pritzker Foundation (www.jb-pritzker.com/page/philanthropy)

## Three Nobel Prizes

James Heckman has made a singular contribution to the world of early nurture through the cultural capital that his Nobel Prize carries. There is something important to be learned from Heckman's work, in conjunction with two other recent Nobel laureates. Muhammad Yunus received the Nobel Peace Prize for his work in global microfinance. Yunus' bold vision was to alleviate poverty not by giving to the poor, but by lending to them – providing essential start-up capital for small business ventures, and the support structure to enable repayment. Yunus' approach treated the poor not merely as objects of pity, but as responsible persons who could participate in a reciprocal relationship of borrowing and repayment. They were not just the recipients of hand-outs; they were people with real human dignity who could, with very modest loans, provide for themselves and their families.

## Muhammad Yunus' Three R's

Three R's characterize Yunus' work: responsibility, respect, and reciprocity. He assumed that the poor could take on the responsibility for a small loan. He offered them the respect and dignity of treating them as meaningful agents of change rather than helpless recipients of aid. And, of course, in the form of a loan, there was built-in reciprocity. It was loan and repayment, not grant and request for another grant. Yunus' innovation and courage is richly deserving of the Nobel Prize he received.

## Al Gore's Inconvenient Truth

Former United States Vice President Al Gore was awarded the Nobel Peace Prize not for a creative approach to poverty alleviation, but for his insistent announcement of *An Inconvenient Truth*. Refusing to be silenced by the political and scientific establishment, Gore raised the profile of global climate change to make it a top-tier issue for virtually every nation on the planet. Like Yunus, he was awarded the Nobel Peace Prize because of his innovation and courage. He simply wouldn't stop preaching his "inconvenient truth."

## What Courageous Innovation Is Needed Now?

The combined work of these three Nobel laureates forms a vortex inviting someone to announce the inconvenient truth about the educational crisis: that parents bear the primary responsibility for the education of their children — and therefore are *the* primary stakeholders in addressing the education crisis. Like Gore's climate change thesis, it is not one that is easily accepted because it challenges the establishment and undermines prevailing assumptions. Like Yunus, it suggests that the way to meaningful change is to respect the dignity of human beings in crisis by treating them as responsible, and entering into a truly reciprocal relationship. It takes the groundbreaking research of James Heckman in economics and applies his maxim that "early advantages accumulate; so do early disadvantages" to the formation of human virtue, and the cultivation of a love of wisdom and learning.

These are the claims which I am venturing; they are contentious and, Seth Godin would (I hope) charge, heretical. My aim is not a Nobel Prize for pioneering fundamental change in addressing the educational crisis any more than Mohammed Yunus was motivated by a Nobel Prize in his work on microfinance. Rather, like Yunus, my motivation is to address a seemingly intractable problem by suggesting that our assumptions are flawed and that a courageous commitment to respectful, reciprocal, responsible relationship is not only innovative but essential to catalyzing real and meaningful educational and social change. Although this is an inconvenient truth, it is the only way to restore the dignity of parents.

# About the Author

Graham Scharf is a father, the husband of a developmental pediatrician, a former *New York City Teaching Fellow*, and co-founder of Tumblon.com.

In 2002, Graham experienced the achievement gap firsthand when he left a rewarding job in an internal consulting team at UBS Financial Services to teach in a failing public school in his neighborhood in Brooklyn, New York. He found teaching 32 third-graders, of whom only one-third began at grade level, even more difficult than his previous experiences living in the bush of rural Uganda. As a teacher, he began asking what had happened that by third grade, the majority of his students could already be one to three years delayed. His research pushed him into early childhood development and the influence of family nurture on health, social justice and educational attainment.

In 2005, Graham put his research and convictions into practice, taking a child-care leave from the Department of Education to provide primary care for his then-eighteen-month-old daughter while his wife continued her medical training in pediatrics, and subsequently developmental pediatrics. At home, he became personally acquainted with first-time parents' need for timely, reliable developmental information in order to know what is normal, what to do, and when to get help. With his lifelong friend, Jonathan Dahl, Scharf co-founded Tumblon.com, the only web app that allows parents to track *their* children's developmental milestones.

Graham lived in New York City for eleven years with his wife and daughters, where he spent most of his time reading, writing, gardening, and exploring playgrounds, parks, libraries, zoos and museums with his daughters. They now live in Charlottesville, Virginia where Graham is helping to launch a small business that provides on-site childcare, parent mentoring, and vocational coaching to its employees: parents of young children.

# ENDNOTES

[i] "Diplomas Count 2009." *Education Week,* 11 June, 2009. Web. 11 Oct. 2009.
<http://www.edweek.org/ew/toc/2009/06/11/index.html>

[ii] "The Condition of College & Career Readiness I 2011" American College Testing Service Annual Report. Retrieved March 28, 2012
http://www.act.org/research/policymakers/cccr11/pdf/ConditionofCollegeandCareerRead iness2011.pdf

[iii] "Closing the Achievement Gap." *The Ounce of Prevention Fund.* 12 Jun. 2009. Web. 18 Jan. 2011.
<http://advocacy.ounceofprevention.org/site/DocServer/ClosingTheAchievementGap0612 2009.pdf?docID=861>

[iv] Tough, Paul. "Whatever It Takes: Geoffrey Canada's Quest to Change Harlem and America." New York: Houghton Mifflin Harcourt. 2009. Print. p104

[v] "A New Generation of Evidence: The Family is Critical to Student Achievement." Henderson, Anne T., Ed.; Berla, Nancy, Ed. [Columbia, Md.] : National Committee for Citizens in Education, 1996, c1994
<http://eric.ed.gov/ERICWebPortal/search/detailmini.jsp?_nfpb=true&_&ERICExtSearch_S earchValue_0=ED375968&ERICExtSearch_SearchType_0=no&accno=ED37598>

[vi] Luscombe, Belinda. "The Fathering Gap: Pitfalls of Modern Fatherhood" Time Magazine: June 15, 2011

[vii] *U.S. Census Bureau, Children's Living Arrangements and Characteristics: March 2002, P200-547, Table C8. Washington D.C.: GPO, 2003. Cited by*
http://www.fatherhood.org/media/consequences-of-father-absence-statistics

[viii] *Source: Hoffmann, John P. "The Community Context of Family Structure and Adolescent Drug Use." Journal of Marriage and Family 64 (May 2002): 314-330. Cited by:*
http://www.fatherhood.org/media/consequences-of-father-absence-statistics

[ix] *Source: America's Children: Key National Indicators of Well-Being. Table SPECIAL1. Washington, D.C.: Federal Interagency Forum on Child and Family Statistics, 1997. Cited by*
http://www.fatherhood.org/media/consequences-of-father-absence-statistics

[x] *Source: Harknett, Kristin. Children's Elevated Risk of Asthma in Unmarried Families: Underlying Structural and Behavioral Mechanisms. Working Paper #2005-01-FF. Princeton, NJ: Center for Research on Child Well-being, 2005: 19-27. Cited by*
http://www.fatherhood.org/media/consequences-of-father-absence-statistics

[xi] *Source: Nord, Christine Winquist, and Jerry West. Fathers' and Mothers' Involvement in Their Children's Schools by Family Type and Resident Status. (NCES 2001-032). Washington, D.C.: U.S. Department of Education, National Center for Education Statistics, 2001. Cited by*
http://www.fatherhood.org/media/consequences-of-father-absence-statistics

[xii] *Source: U.S. Department of Health and Human Services. National Center for Health*

*Statistics. Survey on Child Health. Washington, D.C.: GPO, 1993. Cited by*
http://www.fatherhood.org/media/consequences-of-father-absence-statistics

[xiii] Sanders, R. (2008 2-December). EEGs show brain differences between poor and rich kids. Retrieved 2010 30-December from UC Berkeley News:
http://www.berkeley.edu/news/media/releases/2008/12/02_cortex.shtml

[xiv] Center for Disease Control. (2008 22-October). *Anthropometric Reference Data for Children and Adults: United States, 2003–2006.* Retrieved 2010 30-December from CDC:
http://www.cdc.gov/nchs/data/nhsr/nhsr010.pdf

[xv] Adams, M. J. (1990). *Early Literacy Research Noted in Trainings and Workshops: Every Child Ready to Read.* Retrieved 2010 30-December from American Library Assocation:
http://www.ala.org/ala/mgrps/divs/alsc/ecrr/workshopsab/workshopdescriptions/handre ssources.pdf

[xvi] Hunt, G. (2002). *Honey for a Child's Heart: The Imiginative Use of Books in Family Life.* Grand Rapids: Zondervan.

[xvii] Heckman, J. (n.d.). *Investing in Young Children.* Retrieved 2011 йил 11-January from Heckman Equation:
http://www.heckmanequation.org/system/files/Heckman%20Investing%20in%20Young%2 0Children.pdf

[xviii] Tough, Paul. "Whatever It Takes: Geoffrey Canada's Quest to Change Harlem and America." New York: Houghton Mifflin Harcourt. 2009. Print.

[xix] Hart, B., & Risley, T. R. (2003 Spring). *The Early Catastrophe: The 30 Million Word Gap by Age 3.* Retrieved 2011 18-January from Tree House Learning, Reprint of American Educator v27 n1 p4-9:
http://www.treehouselearning.com/pdf/The_Early_Catastrophe__The_30_Million_Word_ Gap_by_Age3.pdf

[xx] Ferris, H. J. (Ed.). (1957). *Favorite Poems Old and New.* Doubleday.

[xxi] Heckman, J. (2008). *Return on Investment: Costs vs. Benefits.* Retrieved 2010 30-December from Duke University Child and Family Policy:
http://www.childandfamilypolicy.duke.edu/pdfs/10yranniversary_Heckmanhandout.pdf

[xxii] Newbigin, L. (1986). *Foolishness to the Greeks.* Grand Rapids, MI: Eerdmans.

[xxiii] Wright, M. E. (2009 5-January). *All Parents Can Use Support.* Retrieved 2011 8-January from The Huffington Post: http://www.huffingtonpost.com/marian-wright-edelman/all-parents-can-use-suppo_b_155239.html

[xxiv] Ward, K. (2010 26-September). *Who's the Most Important Living New Yorker?* Retrieved 2011 8-January from New York Magazine:
http://nymag.com/news/intelligencer/topic/68530/

[xxv] Harlem Children's Zone. (n.d.). *Our Results.* Retrieved 2010 22-December from Harlem Children's Zone: http://www.hcz.org/our-results

[xxvi] Zigler, E. (2007 April). *The Parents as Teachers program: Its Impact on School Readiness and Later School Achievement.* Retrieved 2011 8-January from Parents as Teachers:
http://www.parentsasteachers.org/images/stories/documents/Executive20Summary_of_ K_Readiness.pdf

[xxvii]Roland J. Fryer http://biography.jrank.org/pages/2961/Fryer-Roland-G.html#ixzz18xbD5me5

[xxviii] Thomson, Gale. "Contemporary Black Biography." Farmington Hills: Biography Resource Center. 2006.

[xxix]Eismeier, T. (2009 5-November). *New Report Reveals That 75% of Young Americans Are Unfit for Military Service.* Retrieved 2011 8-January from Reuters Press Release: http://www.reuters.com/article/idUS205246+05-Nov-2009+PRN20091105

[xxx] Brooks, D. (2009 7-May). *The Harlem Miracle.* Retrieved 2011 8-January from The New York Times: http://www.nytimes.com/2009/05/08/opinion/08brooks.html

[xxxi]Rich, M. (2011 16 April) *The New York Times* Retrieved 2011 17 April from New York Times: http://www.nytimes.com/2011/04/17/weekinreview/17nurture.html?_r=1&emc=eta1&pagewanted=all

[xxxii]Eric A. Finkelstein, J.G. (2009, 27 July) Annual Medical Spending Attributable To Obesity: Payer-And Service-Specific Estimates
*Health Affairs 28*(5) pp. w822-w831

www.ingramcontent.com/pod-product-compliance
Lightning Source LLC
Chambersburg PA
CBHW051840040426
42447CB00006B/631